WHAT PEOPLE A

T0150154

PATHWORKING Т~~нкоυσН Ροεικτ~

Paganism grows from many roots and its profound, numinous, beauty and ready accessibility within the living world around us ensured survival as a strong cultural undercurrent through centuries of religious condemnation. Paganism wells up, of itself, wherever human hearts are open to it. In this wonderful book, Fiona Tinker sets out, analyses, and enters into the spiritual vision implicit in the work of three hugely significant poets; Yeats, MacLeod and O'Sullivan. Her underlying theme is mythopoesis, specifically the ways in which poetry, truly inspired poetry, can connect with us at levels far deeper than the conscious mind can reach. These poems, and the pathworking Fiona Tinker weaves through them, do not tell us what is true. Rather, they inspire and guide us towards thresholds beyond which truth may be found if we are willing to make the journey. Myths need to be entered into rather than received, making *Pathworking Through Poetry* a particularly valuable addition to any thinking Pagan's library.

John Macintyre, former President of The Pagan Federation and former Presiding Officer of the Scottish Pagan Federation.

Here then we have a magical work: From its title of triple meaning through to its challenging use of poetry as a means to tap into the limitless potential of inspiration and on to its invitation to step into the magical cauldron of the bard rather than to remain merely passive. Quite a challenge for the author and the reader both. Fiona Tinker manages the task with great skill, knowledge and the light touch of the fae, that brings a three dimensional experience to a subject that so often manages only two. She reminds us that the bards of old were no mere entertainers, but were, at their best, powerful exponents of an ancient art. This work offers not only an insight into the minds of great poets but also presents a set of tools by which the reader might go forward and discover a new landscape within themselves and a deeper understanding of the relationship between the spirits of nature, mankind and the ancient Celtic gods through the language of poetry. I feel there is much more to come from this author and look forward to discovering it.

Shaun William Hayes, Poet, Druid, co-founder of the Sylvan Grove, member of the Order of Bards, Ovates and Druids (OBOD).

Pagan Portals Pathworking through Poetry:

Visions from the Hearts of the Poets

Pagan Portals Pathworking through Poetry:

Visions from the Hearts of the Poets

Fiona Tinker

MOON
BOOKS

Winchester, UK
Washington, USA

First published by Moon Books, 2012
Moon Books is an imprint of John Hunt Publishing Ltd., Laurel House, Station Approach,
Alresford, Hants, SO24 9JH, UK
office1@jhpbooks.net
www.johnhuntpublishing.com
www.moon-books.net

For distributor details and how to order please visit the 'Ordering' section on our website.

ISBN: 978 1 78099 285 3

A CIP catalogue record for this book is available from the British Library.

Design: Stuart Davies

Printed and bound by CPI Group (UK) Ltd, Croydon, CR0 4YY

We operate a distinctive and ethical publishing philosophy in all
areas of our business, from our global network of authors to
production and worldwide distribution.

CONTENTS

For Iain

Introduction

Paganism is an experiential religion; there is no one sacred text and we are free to find meaning in the ancient texts we find appropriate for our individual paths. Words of wisdom talk to us across time and we can reconstruct ceremony, ritual and observance from them. However, there are also other sources that explore Paganism and the connection between us and the Divine that help to validate our own personal experience. It is through the medium of poetry that others' experiences can feed our own spirituality.

Poetry is a perfect medium to transmit occult teaching. This is not a new idea; it goes back millennia and is one well-known to bards and poets from many eras and traditions. Poetry is full of symbolism, imagery and connotations which pass on meaning. Some of these meanings are clearly apparent and easily recognisable by anyone. However, there are deeper meanings within poems that can be accessed through reflection and meditation, through marrying knowledge of a poem with a wider knowledge of its social, historical and cultural context; and through exploring any folklore allusions in the poem. Those who wish it may learn from the hearts of the poets by taking time to absorb a poem, to uncover the occult knowledge and by doing so, learn much more about what poems have to say.

Sometimes an experiential religion can feel like a lonely place, especially when we first step out on our path. As we learn and develop, meet others and discuss what we have learned, we realise that our personal interactions with the Divine are valid and that – although the paths may be different – our experiences have much in common. This is where an understanding of poetry, of knowing how to read the texts on several levels, comes in. Although some of this may seem like a literature lesson from school – and you may have hated the way literature was taught at school – look again at those literary analysis skills you studied. They really can help you form a Pathworking in your own beliefs and sustain you on your personal spiritual journey.

The approach presented here is to break down each poem into various components: folklore, some literary analysis, exploration of Pagan symbolisms and meanings contained in the poem and suggestions as to how an understanding of the poem can help you explore your own Pagan Pathworking. I've held the opinion for a long time that the Gods and Goddesses choose the humans they want to work with them, and not the other way around; that they choose people who are similar in nature to themselves. Exploring Deities through the illumination inherent in poetry can help us discover who they are – and who we are in their reflected light.

The poems here are from major Scots and Irish writers. All of them unveil a personal meaning from a Celtic perspective.

Literary Analysis

At the heart of any text lies the means to explore what the writer wants us to understand and what they might wish us to take from the text. Not every piece of literature will speak to every person, nor will the same piece speak the same universal truth – the world would be a very boring place if it did. However, good literature leaves us with a feeling of personal involvement, almost as if the writer had transmitted a message directly to us. Within poetry, this message can seem to come straight from the poet's heart to our own. When we find a piece of literature that does have this effect, it is worth investing time to discover what else it might have to tell us.

The conventions of literary analysis that you may recall from school probably look something like this:

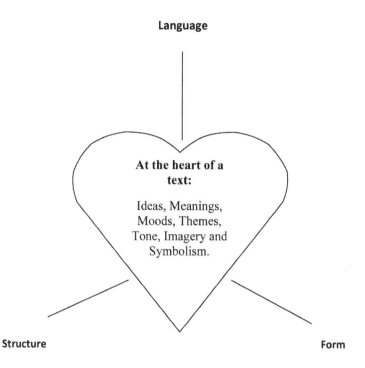

Language

At the heart of a text:

Ideas, Meanings, Moods, Themes, Tone, Imagery and Symbolism.

Structure

Form

Whilst the intention of this book is to look at poetry in some depth, it is not primarily a book about literary criticism, therefore although *some* awareness of literary criticism techniques are useful, the intent really is to explore how poetry can be used as an inspirational tool for Pathworking.

The Poets
WB Yeats

William Butler Yeats (1865-1939) was an Anglo-Irish poet, a prolific writer, a playwright, a politician, a founder of the Abbey National Theatre in Dublin and a member of several esoteric groups, which included membership of the Golden Dawn. He was born in Ireland under British rule and he became a senator in the Irish Parliament when independence from Britain was achieved. Yeats was part of a national revival movement that sought to define what being Irish meant in Irish terms. In his early poetry, Yeats celebrates the heroes of the past, seeking an Irish National Identity through an exploration of mythology and folklore, looking to the stories of Gods and heroes of the past to define Irishness in his present.

Yeats was awarded the Nobel Prize for Literature in 1923.

Fiona MacLeod

Fiona MacLeod was the pen name of William Sharp (1855-1905) a Scottish writer, poet and folklorist who found inspiration in the stories of Gaelic-speaking Scotland. However, to claim that *Fiona MacLeod* was merely a pen name is to underestimate the relationship between Sharp and his muse. She was his alter-ego, his inspiration and, arguably, had an existence of her own on this plane. Sharpe is sometimes credited with popularising the first name *Fiona,* a female form of Fionn, a legendary Celtic hero. The name means 'white' or 'fair'. In addition, her surname links her to the mystical Isle of Skye, home of the MacLeods of fairy descent. Indeed, the fairy legend involving Clan MacLeod of Skye is a very beautiful one and the MacLeods' fairy flag can still be seen at Dunvegan Castle.

Like many writers and artists in the 19th Century, Sharp was a member of the Golden Dawn.

Seumas O'Sullivan

Seumas O'Sullivan was the pen name of James Sullivan Starkey (1879-1958) an Irish poet and visionary. He was born into an Irish Methodist family and his ancestors had stood with Wesley as the Methodism bearing his name was formed. Both grandfathers were ministers. It is from his maternal grandfather – the Rev. James Sullivan – that Starkey took his pen name.

O'Sullivan was the editor of *The Dublin Magazine* and he was friendly with most of the leading luminaries of the Irish Literary Revival. He is possibly the lesser known of the three writers presented here, which is a shame. His poems have a power and a visceral impact that is as equally perceptive and as visionary as Yeats or MacLeod.

O'Sullivan was a Theosophist and he was a member of a Theosophical lodge in Dublin.

Pathworking

Pathworking is a method of interacting with powerful beings and with those who inhabit other realms. It is not for the faint-hearted nor is it for the inexperienced who are uncertain how to protect themselves from anything with a less than honourable intention towards people. William Sharp interacted with Fiona MacLeod in a relationship that was beneficial for them both. Sharp was a member of the Golden Dawn and, as such, had the magical training to know the difference between a genuine woman of the Sidhe and something else that may have spoken with a honey-mouth, but whose intentions were to suck the life-force out of the person who acted as their conduit into this realm. Psychic vampires exist – and not only in this realm. In short, Pathworking should be undertaken with all due regard to psychic self-defence and to the rites and rituals of circle-casting/protection taught within various Pagan traditions. It is not the purpose of this short book to teach psychic self-defence or circle-casting, such matters may be best taught within a Coven, Circle, Hearth or Grove. However, the solitary practi-tioner can find guidance on this within many excellent books. It is taken as a given that anyone embarking upon the Pathworkings suggested here will have made the necessary preparations according to their own tradition.

Thinking in Threes – Why?

Although many traditions call quarters, others use threes and call in the realms of the Land, Sea and Sky. The pattern reflects three main festivals: those of Beltane, Lughnassadh and Samhain, with the pregnant dark time in between. It is also the pattern of the moon. Those who follow this tradition do not ignore the other festivals of the Wheel of the Year or the importance of these to their Pagan kith and kin. However, the other celebrated festivals on the wheel may not hold the same importance for some Pagans as they do for others. This is not a bone of contention or an argument in the making; it is merely a statement of belief that differs from other Pagan practices.

There are three realms: Land, Sea and Sky and the point where they meet is a place out of place – a realm of its own, the liminal space where all three realms meet. It is a place in the Otherworld. People are also in threes: mind, body and soul. There are three ages of man: childhood, maturity and old age. Three is a sacred number in many religions and paths; there is nothing spectacular in the fact some Pagan traditions acknowledge it. The heavy overlay of Roman Catholicism in the life of Ireland and the West Coast of Scotland in previous times masked older beliefs – always useful when the desire is to hide in plain view. Historically, this hiding in plain view may have been a necessity. But the holy trinity of RC belief is merely St Patrick's reworking of the realm of three – or the Druidic Awen, which leads to the liminal space. This veneration of three has its apotheosis in the deeply ancient symbol of the triple spiral, as carved into the great megalithic tomb of Newgrange thousands of years ago.

Working in threes may seem to eliminate Bridget and her festival of Imbolg, but is does not; there is an alternative, significant way of looking at her place in the seasons through the act of her sacred marriage in her role as a fertility Goddess. Brigit is the beautiful consort of Angus (in Scotland) and their sacred marriage marks the spiral dance of the year. The Cailleach Bheur is their opponent and the story of their twice-yearly battle is a powerful metaphor for the liminal transition between the seasons. This is not to say that Brigit is not acknowledged as the important Goddess she is – in all the roles she has as Bridget in Ireland. But she has other attributes in Scotland. The time of her festival is winter still in Scotland; and she has only begun her relationship with Angus as they move towards the rite of the Sacred Marriage. Interestingly, her festival begins as her consort returns to claim her, if the calendar is adjusted for the changes that occurred on the 18th Century. (See the section on Bridget).

A last note about self-protection: whether you call quarters or triples matters not, nor does it matter how you cast your circle of protection. These considerations are entirely down to your own choice and your own training. The important part is to ensure you are protected before Pathworking.

Fiona Tinker
Samhain 2011

Part 1: Poems of Bridget and Angus

Bridget – The Fire in the Head

Bridget is a major Celtic Goddess whose feast is Imbolg, February 1st or February 12/13th, if the old counting is used.[1] Whenever her feast day is celebrated, Bridget is associated with poetry, magic and healing. Here the word *poetry* is used in a much wider sense; Bridget is the Goddess of Divine Inspiration and of Seeing. Inspiration is referred to as the 'fire within the head' – a fitting description of the creative impulse and also of the sensation of using one's psychic ability. Her oversight of magic includes transformation by fire and Bridget is associated with both smiths and the hearth of home. She is also associated with healing, which includes herbalism and midwifery; and of lambing, milk and butter.

Indeed, this Goddess is so important that she could not be banished by the Christian Church and she was absorbed into its pantheon of saints as St Bridget. There are many St Bridgets within the ranks of Catholic saints. One particular St Bridget was the daughter of a 5th C Druid, who converted to Catholicism and established a nunnery in Kildare. This nunnery became famous as a centre of learning; and a lamp was kept lit day and night (an acknowledgement of Bridget as the flame of inspiration?) for this Christian saint, whose feast day, coincidentally, is February 1st.

In the Hebrides, St Bridget is known as the foster mother of Christ, Bridget of the Mantle. This aspect will be discussed further below in MacLeod's *Brigit Speaks*. Bridget is a major Celtic Goddess and too important to be banished to the hinterlands by an incoming religion.

Who better to begin a Pathworking through Poetry with than

8

Bridget, the Goddess of poetry, of seeing and of Divine Inspiration?

The Host of the Air – WB Yeats
Folklore

Yeats's poem *The Host of the Air* was first published in October 1893 under the title of *The Stolen Bride* and the poem retells an ancient story about a bride stolen by the faeries, called the Sidhe in Irish. Yeats heard an old woman singing the tale in Gaelic and she translated it for him. This particular song comes from the Irish oral tradition about faery belief and it tells the story of O'Driscoll, a newly married man, who is glamoured by the Sidhe as they steal away his new bride.

There is a long tradition in Celtic storytelling of the Sidhe stealing people and leaving changelings in their place. These changelings could be sickly faery babies left in place of healthy human babies, or a wife who was not a wife, who had somehow changed her personality. Anyone undergoing such a personality change, whether through physical illness, mental illness, or for some other reason, was considered to have been touched by the Sidhe. This personality change – probably in the form of lethargy or depression – was considered evidence that the real person was 'away with the fairies' and what was left in their place was merely a facsimile of the original. People were considered especially vulnerable to be stolen by the fairies at the times where they were between one state and another: birth, marriage and death. They were people on the edge when in these states and, therefore, more susceptible to unwanted attentions.

There are a variety of legends as to who the Sidhe were and where they came from. The faery realm is sometimes divided into two in Scotland. The Seelie Court is the fae known as the Good Neighbours and they rule from Beltane to Samhain. Their counterpart is the Unseelie Court, whose reign lasts from Samhain to Beltane. The Unseelie Court is the antithesis of the

Good Neighbours. The distinction between the various branches of the fae – or Sidhe – is also to be found in Irish folklore. Early Irish myth cycles tell the stories of the Gods and Goddesses of the *Tuatha De Danaan* and their eventual retreat into the twilight, into the magical places of the borders and edges between our world and theirs. Later stories seem to have an overlay of Catholicism and the stories explain the Sidhe as fallen angels, who were cast out of heaven along with Lucifer. Their crime was the sin of pride and agreeing with Lucifer that they were both the equals of the Christian God and above his puny creation; man. According to this mythos, these fallen angels divided into three groups: those who became the people of the sea, the Merpeople; those who inhabited the land: the Good Neighbours of folklore; and those who inhabited the skies – the Sidhe of the Air. Although there are various legends as to why the Sidhe stole humans, the Sidhe who inhabited the air and rode the winds were considered to hate humans with a passion, because humans had something these Sidhe could never have – a soul. It was for the beauty and purity of their souls that the Hosts of the Air stole brides.

The acknowledged way to reclaim stolen humans was by fire: babies suspected of being changelings were either held over a fire or – in the worse cases – thrown into the fire. The belief was that the faery mother would return the human child in order to save her own child. The ordeal by fire was not limited to babies, but extended to others considered changelings too. As recently as 1895 in Tipperary, a 26-year-old woman, Bridget Cleary, was burned to death by her husband as he was convinced that she was 'away' and what had replaced her was a changeling left by the Sidhe. Needless to say, her husband, Michael Cleary, stood trial for his wife's murder and the story was a high-profile one in Ireland at the time. This occurred at the same time as Ireland was moving towards Home Rule and the juxtaposition of both ensured that Michael Cleary's trial was given a lot of coverage in both Ireland and Britain. Cleary was sentenced to 15 years for manslaughter and upon his release he faded into obscurity, first emigrating to England and then to Canada.

This example of the survival of faery belief occurred when Yeats was a young man just entering his 30s. Yeats had already written **The Stolen Bride** about two years before Bridget Cleary's murder. It is interesting to speculate if the title revision was due in part to sensitivity to the death of Bridget Cleary. However, the point of bringing Bridget Cleary's death and Yeats's poem together is to demonstrate that Yeats's fascination with the folklore of Ireland is evident in his early poetry; and that Bridget Cleary's murder clearly demonstrates a very real survival of faery beliefs among the rural population of Ireland.

On the surface, this poem picks up on this folk belief, where some of the Sidhe are a danger to humanity. The Sidhe have the ability to cast a glamour over humans. The older meaning of *glamour* has nothing to do with its modern usage in terms of celebrities, but is a magic which convinces the enchanted individual that whatever the Sidhe wish them to see is real. The stories of those who found faery gold, only to awake the next morning to a purse full of dead leaves, are examples of faery glamour. Yeats retells the story of the stolen bride to the point where O'Driscoll awakes from his dream-like state and realises his bride has been spirited away. Older versions of the tale have the groom returning to his house to find women keening – lamenting – the death of his young bride. Yet other versions tell of yokes or pieces of wood left in the place of the bride. The groom only realises the deception when the glamour has worn off and he can see what is really there. This clarity of vision is the more obvious meaning in this poem.

This brief summary of faery belief only touches upon the surface of this poem. Yeats's poetry exists on several levels and this poem tells another story, one in keeping with his interest in re-establishing an Irish identity through ancient Celtic lore. And it is one that can be used for Pathworking, to help us reconnect with the Celtic Deities.

The Poem

The Host of the Air

O'Driscoll drove with a song
The wild duck and the drake
From the tall and the tufted reeds
Of the drear Hart Lake.

And he saw how the reeds grew dark
At the coming of night-tide,
And dreamed of the long dim hair
Of Bridget his bride.

He heard while he sang and dreamed
A piper piping away,
And never was piping so sad,
And never was piping so gay.

And he saw young men and young girls
Who danced on a level place,
And Bridget his bride among them,
With a sad and a gay face.

The dancers crowded about him
And many a sweet thing said,
And a young man brought him red wine
And a young girl white bread.

But Bridget drew him by the sleeve
Away from the merry bands,
To old men playing at cards
With a twinkling of ancient hands.

The bread and the wine had a doom,
For these were the host of the air;
He sat and played in a dream
Of her long dim hair.

He played with the merry old men
And thought not of evil chance,
Until one bore Bridget his bride
Away from the merry dance.

He bore her away in his arms,
The handsomest young man there,
And his neck and his breast and his arms
Were drowned in her long dim hair.

O'Driscoll scattered the cards
And out of his dream awoke:
Old men and young men and young girls
Were gone like a drifting smoke;

But he heard high up in the air
A piper piping away,
And never was piping so sad,
And never was piping so gay.
WB Yeats (1899)

Commentary

The poem is set in Hart Lake, also known as Lough Achree, near Sligo, Ireland. Yeats had a special affinity with the landscape around Sligo and he was well-versed in the folktales and fairy belief of the area. Lough Achree is an acknowledged place of magic and myth. This is a wild and beautiful spot, considered to be a place where the veils between the worlds are thin, therefore a place where other worlds connect with ours. The Lough itself is believed to be a portal between the worlds. Setting his poem in this place immediately alerts us to the possibilities of Otherworld activity. The use of the word *drear* is curious: one of its modern meanings is 'mournful' and it indicates what lies ahead for O'Driscoll. It also gives an image of one of those days where the weather is oppressive: a day that feels like humans should not be out in a sacred landscape as the day has been claimed by others. There is a suggestion that a place of outstanding beauty has become depressing and unpleasant.

O'Driscoll is on the lands around Lough Achree and he drives the wild ducks from the lake with his song. We are not told if this is deliberate, as in he was hunting wild duck for food, or whether he was just making a lot of tuneless noise that disturbed the birds and caused offence to the Sidhe. However, if we consider hunting more likely, this may have been the cause of the offence. Hart Lake is a watery entrance to another world. Perhaps the Sidhe considered the ducks that lived around the lake as their own animals. Ducks, like swans, traverse the three realms of land, sea and sky and in this sense they are birds of special significance. If O'Driscoll is poaching from the Sidhe, he is about to pay a high price for the stolen birds.

As night begins to fall, O'Driscoll's thoughts turn to Bridget, his new wife. (We can assume she is his new wife from the use of the word *bride*.) He is now in a dangerous place, in the time that is neither day nor night, the twilight time, the: 'coming of night-tide'. As he dreams of Bridget and her 'long dim hair' the twilight people, in the form of the Sidhe of the Air, begin to work their mischief and cast a glamour over him. *Dim* is a strange word to use about someone's hair, the connotations are dark, unshining and lank – all of which create an unattractive image and add to the oppressive atmosphere of the poem. What could be so special about someone with hair like that? Yet Yeats repeats this phrase in the poem; it matters, as we will discover later.

The theme of depression is continued as he hears the faery

music – but this faery music is not joyful, it has a bitter-sweet sound to it: 'and never was piping so sad, and never was piping so gay'. Even the music is in a twilight state, it is neither one thing nor the other. O'Driscoll finds himself under its spell, he *dreamed*. The word is repeated twice to emphasise the glamour he is now under as a result of hearing the piper play. Suddenly, he is aware of dancers and 'Bridget his bride' dancing amongst them.

O'Driscoll is surrounded by the dancers, who flatter him and offer him red wine and bread. There are connotations of the Christian mass within this imagery and it is interesting to speculate that one of the purposes of the offering was almost a parody of the mass – on a much deeper level this could be interpreted as the Sidhe seeking revenge for the people of Ireland turning from their old beliefs. 'The bread and the wine had a doom, For these were the Hosts of the Air' is a fascinating quotation to contemplate in this respect. The Anglo-Saxon meaning of the word *doom* is 'judgement' and 'law'. Taken in the sense of judgement, it can be considered that the Sidhe do pass judgement on the belief system that banished them to the hinterlands, to myth and to story. Then again, *doom* in the sense of law relates back to old Celtic mythology: anyone who eats or drinks whilst in the land of the fae is trapped and very few return from the realm of the Sidhe having done so. O'Driscoll is saved from this fate by Bridget who: 'drew him by the sleeve' to join a card game. However, she cannot save him from the doom, in its modern usage of an unhappy end, awaiting him.

Bridget pulls O'Driscoll away from the dancers to play a game of chance with old men. This game is not what it seems as the oxymoron contained in: 'a twinkling of ancient hands' indicates. Elderly hands are generally arthritic and slow; they are not usually capable of making movements that could be described as *twinkling* – an onomatopoeic word more associated with deft, swift movement. O'Driscoll is glamoured, he sees what the Sidhe want him to see, elderly men playing cards. This is a game he cannot win on any level, he is being cheated.

O'Driscoll remains in his dream-like state, oblivious to the bad luck awaiting him – until a handsome young man carries Bridget away from the dance. The young man's body is 'drowned' by Bridget's 'long dim hair'. Her hair – unattractive as it might sound – has significance for both O'Driscoll and the man of the Sidhe. The sight of the Bridget – and her hair – in the arms of a stranger is enough to snap O'Driscoll out of his glamoured state and he awakes, throwing the cards around as he does so. Suddenly, all the dancers disappear – as does Bridget. All that is left to O'Driscoll is the sound of bitter-sweet fairy music as the piper pipes the Host of the Air away from Hart Lake.

There is an additional possible interpretation of the poem that leads us into the link between old and new religions and to Pathworking that can help you discover the Celtic Goddess Bridget.

If O'Driscoll is read as a metaphor for Christianity, he drives 'the wild duck and the drake' i.e. women and men from a sacred site 'with a song' – perhaps a hymn. The new religion is determined to take over an ancient place which has doorways to the Otherworld associated with it. The word choice *wild* would imply that the behaviour of the people is not acceptable to the mores of the incoming religion and such behaviour would need to be 'tamed'. It is a fact that Christianity built many of its early churches on Pagan sacred sites – perhaps the early proponents of that faith proselytised around Sligo and the meaning of Hart Lake was becoming forgotten, moving from the realms of the Gods to that of folk belief. Perhaps this is what Yeats hints at by describing the lake as *'drear'* – the Otherworld beings who inhabit this place are angry that they have been forgotten. Bridget the Goddess is often depicted and described in flame; her hair is red, fiery and bright. One interpretation of Yeats's repetition of 'her long dim hair' could be the dimming of knowledge and worship of the Goddess Bridget, who has been replaced by a multitude of St Bridgets, embodying various aspects of the Goddess. The Goddess is *'long dim'* and only survives in folk song, mixed up with the Christian interpretation of the Sidhe. One of the variations of Bridget's name is *Bride* – Yeats makes a pun with the original title of this poem: *The Stolen Bride*. The Goddess Bridget had indeed been stolen by the church and the fires of inspiration, as personified by her flaming hair, were dimmed. *'Long dim'* is not just a physical description of the Goddess; it can be read as a reference to the centuries of forgetfulness that attempted to turn Bridget into a saint of another religion.

Yeats's poem is a retelling of folk belief about the Sidhe stealing humans and leaving changelings in their place. It can also be read as a short exploration of what has been lost by the fracturing of the Goddess Bridget into a variety of St Bridgets, each personifying just one aspect of a major Celtic Deity. Moreover, the repetition of 'long dim hair' is a meditation point useful for entering into Pathworking.

Brigit Speaks – Fiona MacLeod/William Sharp
Folklore

In Scotland, Bridget is often written as Brigit, and alternatives of this are Bride, Brede and Bridie. She is worshipped in all her aspects familiar to those who worship her in Ireland. However, there are several additional attributes of the Scottish Brigit that have led to some speculation that this Goddess is not the same as the Irish Bridget. There are enough similarities to consider them the same Goddess and to speculate that the differences in attributes are possibly geographical or that the social-historical differences between Ireland and Scotland have resulted in a difference of focus.

In Scottish myth, Brigit has a role as the rescued bride, the Goddess of Spring. Her sacred marriage to Angus Òg is the event that signals the start of summer. Without her, the return of spring will not happen. In this aspect, she is seen as an Earth Goddess, a mother, and their sacred marriage at Beltane heralds the beginning of summer. In the following story, Brigit is referred to as Bride: myth has it that she is captured by the Goddess of Winter, the Cailleach, who does not want her reign as Queen of Winter to end. The following is a simplified *retelling* of this myth from Donald MacKenzie's 1917 folklore collection **Scottish Wonder Tales from Myth and Legend.**[2]

Beira is the Cailleach, the crone Goddess of Winter. It is she who washes her cloak in the Corryvrecken whirlpool in the Sound of Jura and spreads it out on the hills to dry. As she does so, snow covers the land. Storms and winds accompany her reign. The Cailleach does not want to relinquish her crown and she keeps Bride, the Princess of Spring, captive in an attempt to prolong her rule.

In the winter months, Angus Òg lived on the Green Isle of the West, the Land of Youth. This is a floating Isle that many sailors have lost their lives in searching for. It is an Island, always to the west whether you are in Scotland or Ireland. It is not Tir Na Nog, nor any of the other realms of the Gods. It is a retreat of the Gods, ruled sometimes by the Dagda, sometimes by a figure simply called the King of the Green Isle and Angus's father.

Angus first saw Bride in a dream and he fell in love with her. In his dream, he spoke to an old man and asked why Bride wept. 'She weeps because she is the prisoner of the Cailleach, and Beira treats her cruelly.'

When Angus woke, he told the King of the Green Isle about his dream.

The King of the Green Isle answered, 'The fair princess you saw is Bride and in the days when you will be King of the Summer, she will be your queen.'

Immediately, Angus wanted to set off to Scotland to rescue Bride, but the King of the Green Isle advised caution:

'It is the wolf-month. Remember how dangerous the wolf is.'

Angus answered, 'Then I shall cast a spell on the sea and a spell on the land and borrow for February three days from August.'

He did this and the ocean slept gently and the sun shone. Angus mounted his white horse and rode eastwards to Scotland, crossing the Minch and reaching the Grampians as dawn broke. Angus searched all over Scotland, but he could not find Bride anywhere.

Bride too, dreamt and her dreams told her that Angus searched for her. She was happy as she knew her time with Beira was coming to an end.

However, Beira was angry that Angus sought to free Bride and on the third evening of his visit, she raised a great storm that blew Angus back to the Green Isle. But he returned – and each time he returned, Beira again raised a storm that blew him back to the Island.

Then came the day when Angus found Bride. When they spoke to one another, the birds sang and the sun shone. Bride was transformed and that is why this day is called Bride's day – February 13th, the first day of spring.

Angus and Bride were married. The Sidhe sang with joy and the shepherds declared that spring had come. Bride and Angus walked over the land. She waved her hands, weaving her magic and Angus sang his spells, weaving his magic – and the land grew green and beautiful. All the people in Scotland felt their presence in the land and looked to the coming spring.

Beira was angered when she knew that Angus had found Bride. She raised her magic hammer and struck the earth until it had frozen solid again. Yet the birds still sang of the sacred marriage and Bride and Beira knew her reign was coming to an end. She called her hag servants together and bid them wage war on Angus. She herself mounted her black steed and set off in pursuit of Angus.

Angus and Bride fled to the island in the west and passed many happy days together. However, he longed to return to Scotland and reign as the King of Summer. Again and again, Angus crossed the sea and each time he reached the land, the sun broke out and the *birds sang to welcome him.*

Beira raised storm after storm to drive him away. Many times this war waged between them and the power of winter drove him back to the west. And time and time again, Angus returned. Beira took back the three August days that Angus borrowed for February and used them to freeze the land. People suffered, animals died and the early crops shrivelled in the cold. Angus felt sorry for mankind, but he knew that Beira's reign must end.

Beira knew it too. She waited until the dawn of that day when day and night are of equal length, and then she travelled to the Green Isle and drank from the waters of youth. And on that day Angus began his reign as King of Summer, with Bride at his side, as his queen.

Anyone who has lived in the north of Scotland will recognise the weather patterns, including the *general* pattern of three nice February days that are then countered by some lively August weather. In MacKenzie's tale, the turning of the year depends on the sacred marriage between a God and a Goddess, Angus and Bride.

In Irish myth, Angus's dream is of a girl whom he falls in love with. In brief, he began to waste away pining for her and eventually, the girl of his dream was identified as Caer Ibormeith, a princess of Connacht (see later section about Angus.) Her father objected to Angus's suit, but eventually agreed he could marry her, if he could identify her from her handmaidens. This was trickier than expected – Caer changed into a swan at Samhain and remained this way either for a year or six months, depending on which version of the myth you read. However, Angus had no problem picking her out from all the other swans and if her father thought a fanfare of feathers was likely to put Angus off the idea of marrying his daughter, he was sadly mistaken. Angus transformed himself into a swan so he could be with Caer.

There are shared elements in the two stories: Angus has a

dream of the woman he wants to marry and he sets off in search of her. He encounters many difficulties on the way and, eventually, he achieves his goal. The Irish tale of Angus's marriage to Caer does not carry the connotations of the Sacred Marriage that the Scottish tale does. Brigit/Bride is the Goddess of the Land, the Goddess of Fertility, and without her marriage to Angus, the summer will not return and the land will remain barren. The Scottish tale reveals additional aspects of the fertility and creativity of Bridget.

Fiona MacLeod, herself arguably a woman of the Sidhe, honours Bridget in all her aspects and names in her poem, as she understood them. However, before exploring MacLeod's poem, it is worth exploring Macleod herself.

Fiona MacLeod

On a very superficial level, Fiona MacLeod was merely the pen-name of the Scottish folklorist and occultist, William Sharp. He arguably chose a female name to allow him to write in a more feminine style than in his writing as a man. However, Fiona was much more than just a *nom de plume* and she did seem to have an existence in another place, a twilight place. It seems that Sharp was attuned to her – and she to him. He channelled her and she was his muse.

Fiona MacLeod's surname alludes to links with Skye. Her surname is certainly long-linked with that island, but that is not the only interesting point in her antecedents. The MacLeods are an ancient and powerful Scottish clan and their family seat is at Dunvegan Castle, Isle of Skye. One of the treasures held within their castle is an ancient flag – *Am Bratach Sith*, the faery flag. *Sith* is Scots Gaelic for faery, a feminine form of the word, pronounced the same as Sidhe. It can also mean *reconciliation* and *peace*. However, the faery flag is no old battle trophy proudly displayed, but a gift from the Sidhe to protect Clan MacLeod in times of need. The MacLeods of Dunvegan are in part Sidhe and this is how it came about. A long time ago, a MacLeod Chief married a woman of the Sidhe. Her people were not pleased at this, but they gave her leave to remain at Dunvegan for a year and a day. However, the condition was that when she returned to them, she could bring nothing from the human world. Sadly, this included the little son born to her during her time at the castle. On the night of a feast to celebrate the birth of their son, MacLeod and his wife had to part, she to return to her home.

The child was left in the care of a nursemaid during the celebrations. MacLeod had instructed the nursemaid not to leave the child alone, but she disobeyed this in order to hear some of the music playing in the great hall below. Whilst the baby was alone, he woke up and began to cry. No-one came to comfort him and his crying reached the ears of his mother in the twilight place. She could not return in body, so she sent her spirit through the portal between her world and ours in order to comfort her son. The baby's mother wrapped him in green blanket and soothed her son.

In the meantime, the Chieftain had discovered that the nursemaid had abandoned her post and sent her to fetch his son immediately, to ensure he was safe. The nursemaid returned with the child and, as she came into the hall, ethereal faery music began to play. Suddenly, a song of prophecy filled the air: the blanket around the child was a faery flag and it would keep the MacLeods safe. It could be waved in battle and the battle would be won in their favour. However, it could only be used three times. To date, it has been used twice and both times the prophecy has held true. This is how the MacLeods of Dunvegan came to have faery ancestry and why their faery flag is treasured.

All nuances of the word *sith* are evident in the beautiful tale of *Am Bratarch Sith*, which is about MacLeod and the love of a faery woman for her half-human son. When Fiona MacLeod announced herself to William Sharp, her antecedents as a woman of the Sidhe were more than evident in her surname.

The Poem

Brigit Speaks

I am older than Brigit of the Mantle,
I put songs and music on the wind
Before ever the bells of the chapels
Were rung in the West
Or heard in the East.
I am Brighid-nam-Bratta:
Brigit of the Mantle,
I am also Brighid-Muirghin-na-tuinne:
Brigit, Conception of the Waves,
And Brighid-sluagh,
Brigit of the Faery Host,
Brighid-nan-sitheachseang,
Brigit of the Slim Faery Folk,
Brigid-Binne-Bheule-
Ihuchd-nan-trusganan-uaine,
Brigit the Melodious Mouthed
Of the Tribe of the Green Mantles.
And I am older than Aone (Friday)
And as old as Luan (Monday)
And in Tir-na-h'oige my name is
Suibhal: Mountain Traveller,
And in Tir-fo-thuinn, Country of the Waves,
It is Cu-gorm: Gray Hound,
And in Tir-na-h'oise,
Country of Ancient Years,
It is Sireadh-thall: Seek Beyond.
And I have been a breath in your heart,
And the day has its feet to it
That will see me coming
Into the hearts of men and women
Like a flame upon dry grass,

Like a flame of wind in a great wood.[3]
Fiona MacLeod (1895)

Commentary

MacLeod's beautiful poem is both a devotional and a promise. It communicates two ways: from the Otherworld to this world and back again; much like the relationship between MacLeod and Sharp. The Scots Gaelic and the English are woven together to ensure that all that Brigit was, is and will be is completely understood. It ends with Brigit's promise to return and re-ignite the fire in the head and the heart. It is a song of the Sidhe and it is for us to find the tune. The poem is deceptively simple, but an exploration of the imagery in the poem leads to a greater understanding of Brigit.

The poem begins *'I am older than Brigit of the Mantle'*. This is a categorical reference to the Highland belief that St Brigit was the foster-mother of Christ and had wrapped the new-born infant in her cloak. The persona of Brigit in this poem makes it clear that she is an older being, much older than the St Brigit of the foster-mother story. This is a straightforward interpretation of the words used, but further reflection reveals links to understanding Brigit the Goddess. *Mantle* denotes a cloak, as is intended in the obvious reference in this poem. However, the word has other meanings and connotations, including the covering over the household fire and the layer between the surface of the earth and its fiery centre. *Mantle* has connotations of a protective layer between fire and another state. Brigit is telling us that she is our protector – literally, too much fire will kill: metaphorically, too much inspiration or psychic ability will drive us mad, causing us to burn up and burn out. History is full of examples of prophets and poets who were *too* good at what they did and who burnt out too early. Brigit protects us from this, her mantle is a shield.

Brigit's mantle is green in myth and the stories contained within myth are beautiful. For example, in Ella Young's **Celtic**

Wonder Tales[4] the story of the creation of the earth from chaos is through Brigit and her mantle, in the sense of mantle as a cloak. Brigit hears the chaos that is the earth sing a longing-song of beauty and peace. She convinces the other Gods to accompany her to the earth as she wishes to make the longing-song a reality. They do so and from chaos bring forth the earth. Brigit lays her green mantle over the earth and this becomes the land, beloved of Brigit. Angus adds beauty and shape to the landscape. This love of the earth dovetails with her role as Goddess of the Land in Scotland and the joint shaping of the earth with Angus foretells their sacred marriage.

The first stanza of MacLeod's poem emphasises how old Brigit is: she was here long before the Christian church came to the west – or even to the east. She is *Brighid-nam-Bratta* – Brigit of the Mantle; she cloaks the earth and all it holds within her protection. She was the song on the wind in the time of creation. Indeed, MacLeod tells us that she is older than creation: '*And I am older than Aone (Friday)/And as old as Luan (Monday)*'. This allusion is to the Biblical story of Genesis and would be readily understood in the context of Sharp's late Victorian audience.

The persona in the poem continues to state who she is and what her names are in the realms of the Sidhe. Meditation on her names, in conjunction with the realm they belong to, will enable the seeker to know Brigit, as will studying MacLeod's writings. In brief, Brigit tells us that she is called '*Suibhal: Mountain Traveller*' in Tir-na-h'oige, the Land of Eternal Youth. This land is a magical realm, where beauty and music rule. It is not accessible to humans unless they have an invitation and a guide from the Sidhe. Brigit is: '*Cu-gorm: Gray Hound*' in Tir-fo-thuinn, The Land under Waves. This is the realm of the selkies and the sea-people. It is also the realm where – in some stories – Brigit sought her lost brother, Manannan Mac Lir. In Tir-na-h'oise, the Land of Ancient Years, Brigit is known as: '*Sireadh-thall: Seek Beyond*'. All of these titles are poetry in the mouth that waits to be spoken, but they also mean something much deeper. Their connotations and imagery tells us how powerful this Goddess is, her realms reach across time and space, from the beginning to the end of a human lifespan and her presence is with us in every step of that journey. In this poem, Brigit tells us she is the guide who will invite us to her realm to *seek beyond* our own existence.

MacLeod's poem continues to give titles for Brigit, each of which places her as a Goddess of the earth – of the Land, the Sea and the Sky. She is the earth-singer and: *'Brigit of the Faery Host'*. Nothing could be plainer or simpler in MacLeod's statements of Brigit's attributes. It is worth considering that the *Am Bratarch Sith* was said to be originally green, as is Brigit's mantle. This gives another level of meaning to the story of the MacLeod flag – who exactly *was* the Sidhe wife of Malcolm MacLeod?

It has been mooted that Fiona MacLeod was herself a manifestation of Brigit, speaking through William Sharp. If this is so, then it is also possible that an earlier excursion into this world by Fiona was as the faery bride of MacLeod of Dunvegan. All of this is merely speculation, but thought-provoking conjecture all the same.

As a devotional, this poem is meant to be sung or spoken aloud. Brigit states she is: *'Brigit the Melodious Mouthed/Of the Tribe of the Green Mantles'*. The alliteration of *Melodious Mouthed* suggests that music should accompany the words. But, as humans, we do not possess the tune. However, there is a clue to finding the melody and it lies in the rhythm of the poem: many of the English lines are written in iambic pentameter. This is a pattern of five stressed and five unstressed syllables in a line, which echoes the human heartbeat. The clue to finding the song lies within our own hearts.

There is another clue as to how the poem may be sung and that lies in the harmonics, lilts and inflections of Scottish Gaelic. Gaelic does not follow English patterns of speech and it is a musical language on the ear, with soft sounds and uplifting intonations on words that do not translate when the language is anglicised. If the poem is read with Gaelic inflections – with even the English words given Gaelic speech patterns – the song is almost there. What is in the seeker's heart will supply the rest of the tune. It is suggested that the Gaelic of Skye is used, should you wish to try this invocation: there are differences in Gaelic speech among the Isles. Fiona MacLeod is linked with Skye, so it would seem to make sense to use the Gaelic she knew.

The poem concludes with Brigit's promise: she will return:

And the day has its feet to it
That will see me coming
Into the hearts of men and women
Like a flame upon dry grass,
Like a flame of wind in a great wood.

The last stanza is completely in English: perhaps this is so that her message is unequivocally understood by all of MacLeod's readers. The expressions are those of a Gaelic speaker: *'and the day has its feet to it'*, which give the poem an authentic voice. Her promise concludes with two similes, both invoking the imagery of rekindling fire. This imagery may appear destructive: flames through dry grass and woods will ignite and be destroyed. On one level, this image works because after such destruction comes new growth, an awakening of the powers of creation. On another level, reading the similes as figurative language suggests imagery of a burst of fire within the head: the gift of inspiration bestowed by Brigit.

Pathworking
Meditative Tools

Light a candle in the middle of your circle and place a drawing you have made of the triple spiral from the entrance to Newgrange, Co. Meath. This triple spiral will reveal its inner secrets to you through meditation and reflection. Its symbolism is ancient; the spiral is created in one smooth movement, calling to mind the flow of time and water. The symbol of the triple spiral echoes in triples: land, sea and sky; birth, death and rebirth; above, here, and below. However the spiral echoes with you, it will be in a way that flows, one thing leading smoothly to another and then back again without interruption.

Cast your circle and make the honours to your Gods and/or ancestors as you normally would. Call on Bridget and declare your wish to know her and your intent to honour her in whichever aspect she considers you are best placed to work with her. Ask Bridget to grant you an audience. Take your time with this – open your heart and be honest in your intent. If your wish is one-way, i.e. you merely want Bridget to grant you something, such as creativity or seeing, do not be surprised if you are ignored. *Sireadh-thall* is more than one of Brigit's titles, it is a two-way thing and the truth of the heart cannot be hidden from her.

If you have explored *Brigit Speaks* and have a tune for it, sing this song of the Sidhe in honour of Brigit in all her aspects. If no song came to you, chant the poem instead. The intention is to honour Brigit by speaking or singing her names aloud.

Place the triple spiral in front of the candle and focus on the candle flame. See the spiral begin to spin and to flow. Take slow, even breaths and allow yourself to begin your journey, to the essence of Yeats's poem. In your mind's eye, see O'Driscoll gamble whilst his bride dances with the Hosts of the Air. Do nothing but watch for a while, as the scene becomes clearer and real. Should the dancers observe you, do nothing to offend them, make a bow then remain still. Do not eat or drink, if offered refreshment – and do not join the dance if requested to do so by any other than Bridget. Your purpose here is to observe, to learn from O'Driscoll and to learn from the sadness of Ireland, of what happens when people start to forget. Observe Bridget's 'long dim hair' and picture it becoming brighter, redder and more beautiful as you honour this Goddess. See her in all her glory; imagine her as the fire in the head. Your purpose is to see what is really there and to learn how to break the glamour of the Hosts of the Air. Do not be fooled by old men with twinkling hands. Such things are not possible – look, then look again. Note all that you see: the colours, the background, the manner of clothing and so forth. All of this will have personal significance for you.

At this point, Bridget may well notice you standing at the edges and invite you to dance. It is safe to do so and Bridget has honoured you. As you dance, listen and speak to her with your heart, not your head. You cannot alter O'Driscoll's story, but you can alter your own. Listen to Bridget. She has noticed you.

You will not stay until the end of the dance as you have used O'Driscoll's tale to enter the Otherworld to observe the story and to learn about the Hosts of the Air. Bridget will leave you once again at the edges of the dance; it is time to take your leave. Bow to the dancers of the Sidhe and slowly bring yourself back from the dance, to the place where the candle flame burns and the spiral pattern dances. Hold Bridget in your heart – and see her hair begin to glow again.

With this image of Bridget in mind, focus again on the spiral and begin to sing or chant MacLeod's poem. Do this according to the song in your heart, not one that has been taken from another. It does not matter if you are tuneless; the music is in the words. Continue this and watch the spiral begin to flow.

You will find yourself elsewhere. What form this elsewhere takes will depend on the aspect of you that Bridget sees as your strength. If you are a craftsperson, you may find yourself in a forge, beside a fire. If you are a poet or a seer, you may find yourself at the start of a path through beautiful woodland. If you are a homemaker, you may find yourself with a babe in arms. If you are a farmer, you may find yourself surrounded by ewes at lambing. The manifestations of Bridget are as varied as her attributes. If Bridget has chosen you to work with her, there will be a part of you that is a part of her and she will emphasise this to you in this Pathworking through the signs and symbols she chooses to share with you. Pay attention to what to see, what you hear and what you feel. All of these are the tools you will need in this world to honour her and work with her.

Once you are in your specified location, relax. Take the time to look. Feel the textures of any objects around you; don't just note what they are. Suddenly, you will be aware of a presence. Bridget is there – in all her shining, fiery-headed glory. See her. Concentrate on the brightness of her hair. Do not be afraid. She has a message for you – listen, don't speak. Absorb what she says. If you think that what she says is a bit out of kilter with how you perceive yourself, think again. Her last given title is *Seek Beyond* and this is what she may advise you to do – to develop those parts of yourself that you were only dimly aware existed. It is time for you to ignite your own metaphorical *long dim hair*. She has chosen you as one of her followers, honour this.

The manifestation fades and you will find yourself back in this reality, looking at the candle flame, watching the spiral turn. Breathe quietly and reflect on what you have learned. Slowly return to full consciousness in this plane. When you are ready, close your circle, give thanks to those due it – and give thanks to Bridget.

Once this small ritual is complete, you will probably be really hungry. This is normal; it takes a lot of energy to walk the worlds in a Pathworking. Eat, and then write in your journal. Over the following days, incorporate what you have learned into your everyday life. This is one way to honour Bridget. Another is to use whatever advice she gave you, complete any requests she made and develop your latent gifts as Bridget has suggested.

Angus Òg - The Laughter in the Heart

Most people will have heard of Angus Òg in the context of his position as the Irish God of love, music and poetry. His name is variously written Aenghus, Oengus, Aonghus, Aengus and Angus, but for simplicity, I will use Angus, unless using direct quotation. He is the younger son of the Dagda and the Goddess, Boann, for whom the River Boyne is named. Boann was the wife of Elcmar of Newgrange in Co. Meath. Irish myth tells us that the Dagda desired Boann so much, he sent her husband, Elcmar, to a distant part of his kingdom whilst he made love to Boann. When she conceived, the Dagda caused time to stand still; therefore Angus was conceived, gestated and born in one day. According to this version, it is from being born in time that is no time that his name arises: he is the 'ever young'. The Irish sources tell many tales of Angus; and the more familiar ones are those about him in his guise as the God of Love. He owned a harp that played such sweet music that all who heard it could not help but follow him. He was surrounded by four white birds, which were his kisses. All of this makes a very pretty tale, but it does not do justice to Angus as a major Celtic God.

There are many other aspects to Angus, in both Ireland and Scotland, which may be less familiar. One tale relates that after Angus' birth, the Dagda took him to Midir to be fostered. As a child, Angus was oblivious to his origins until he was taunted by another child about not having parents. When he questioned Midir, Angus learned that the Dagda was his father and Boann his mother.

He later demanded a house of his own and the Dagda helped him trick Elcmar out of Newgrange. At the feast of Samhain, Angus asked Elcmar if he could be master of the house for a day and a night. Elcmar agreed to this and departed, leaving Angus as master of Newgrange. Oaths, vows and promises made at

Samhain were held even more sacred than usual in a society where a man's word was his bond. Elcmar gave in gracefully when he realised how Angus had tricked him: there is no indefinite article in Irish and Angus asking to live in Newgrange 'for day and night' meant that Elcmar had agreed for him to live there for all time. Such a story indicates an aspect of Angus as a trickster, sharp-witted, quick-thinking and able to change his situation to great advantage. This adds more depth to his character than the regretfully shallow but common portrayal of him as some kind of Celtic Eros.

However, as all Gods have complex aspects and contradictory qualities, so does Angus. He is gentle, quiet and hangs in the background, not one to push himself to the fore – unless necessary. Love, music and poetry are also his passions. Moreover, he is an 'Ever-Young' God – but this is not the same as being 'young'. Picture him as a man in his mid to late-twenties, not as some kind of pre-pubescent cherub, as depicted in some paintings. As mentioned above, he is said to have four white birds that fly around his head that were formed from his kisses. Some oral sources say that should a wagtail land in front of you and look pleased to see you, Angus has sent you a kiss. The mountain ash – the rowan (rodden in Scots) is sacred to him. He has the ability to transform and shape-shift, usually into the form of a white swan, but some stories tell of other transformations. At various times, he has become a white stag, various white birds and as a large purple and pink fly.

Angus has other concerns: he is the centre of the spiral and he is the keeper of the keys to the realms, making him a God of Life, Death and Rebirth. He is a seller of dreams – and a bringer of nightmares. He is a trickster and a frightener. Many of the old Scottish tales expand on these darker traits, sometimes mentioning a shadowy called Dark Angus.

Angus may be young, but he is no fool. Many of the old tales gathered by the Scottish Literary Revivalists show a Deity who is hope eternal, the joy of life, a God above the other Gods. The following re-telling of Fiona MacLeod's beautiful story about Angus Òg illustrates this point: the world has neither love nor laughter without him.

The Awakening of Angus Òg[5]

One day, among the hills and mountains, and nestled in the gold and purple heather, Angus Òg lay sleeping in a tarn. The tallest growing thing on the mountainside was a mountain ash, growing half way up the side of the mountain. It leaned to in such a way that the sun danced from its leaves and branches, no matter which direction it shone from. It was a beautiful tree and it was under this rowan that Angus dreamt. The mountain, Ben Monach, stood as guard of the mountain slope where the tree grew; and Angus slept on and the peace of the earth protected him.

Three old Druids came over the brow of the hill and walked slowly to where Angus dreamed. However, these were not three old Druids, but three of the Ancient Gods. They sought to wake Angus, but Angus had the breath of the granite across him – and he slept on, undisturbed by the three Gods' attempts to wake him.

'Awake,' cried Keithor, and his voice was that of the wind through the forest and the song of the wind in the grass.

'Awake,' cried Manannan, and his voice was the boom of the sea against the shore.

'Awake,' cried Aesus, and his voice was the life and pulse of the world carried in the wind.

Angus Òg dreamed on. He dreamed of the creation of the worlds, of sending his laughing, summer song dancing across them. He dreamed of dancing, silver rain that fell on many forests and green places. He dreamed of the four harping winds of this world. He dreamed of the four white birds that are his kisses following the winds and he dreamed he sent his kisses flitting through the shadows.

'He will awake no more,' sighed Keithor and the mourning of the

God of the green world was the sad sigh of the wind lamenting through the reeds and grasses.

'He will awake no more,' sighed Manannan, and the mourning of the God of the seas was the gentle sounds of the waves lamenting against the shores of the Isle of the Dead.

'He will awake no more,' sighed Aesus, and the mourning of the Unseen God was the soughing of the grass and the dimming of the sun.

Angus Òg had the deep age of the granite upon him and he slept as the dead do. But the Ancient Ones were so ancient; they did not see eternity at rest. They forgot that Angus is the God of Youth and only he is eternal and unchanging. Sadly, they walked away.

Winter turned to summer and back again. A thousand years passed. Once again, the three Ancient Gods came onto the mountainside.

'Awake Angus,' they cried, 'for the world has need of you and it has grown cold and chill.' They had the grey grief upon them as they stood in the silence as Angus dreamt on.

Then the birds spoke:

'Keithor, answer me this. If death came to you, what would happen?'

'The green world would wither and die, the wind would blow without purpose and the crops shrivel,' replied the God of the Land.

'Manannan, answer me this. If death came to you, what would happen?'

'The seas would run dry, sand would fall instead of dew and the world would fall into the abyss,' answered the God of the Sea.

'Aesus, answer me this. If death came to you, what would happen?'

'There would be no heartbeat at the heart of the earth, no lift of star against sun, all would be darkness and silence,' answered the God of the Sky.

The doves were pleased with these answers. They responded thus, 'Yet Angus Óg has slept the sleep of a thousand years and none knew it. For a thousand years, the beating of his heart of love has been the beating of the world. For a thousand years his breath has been the coming of spring in the human heart. For a thousand years the breath of his life has been warm against the lips of lovers. These memories have been sweet against oblivion.'

'Who is he?' asked Keithor. 'Is he older than I, who saw the green earth born?'

'Who is he?' asked Manannan. 'Is he older than I, who saw the first waters pour forth from the void?'

'Who is he?' asked Aesus. 'Is he older than I, who saw the first comet wander from the starry fold, who saw the first moon and who felt the heat of the first sun?'

'He is older!' sang the birds. 'He is the soul of the Gods!' And with that, they fanned a wind with their wings and took away the deep sleep that was upon Angus.

Angus awoke, and laughed across the land. With his laughing, the whole green earth was covered in blossom. And Angus arose and smiled. With his smiling, the old brown world dressed itself in dewy green and the world became beautiful. The pulse of love leapt in beating hearts. Angus Òg walked in the sunlight, weaving rainbows and dreams, spreading a wild, glad joy as he walked.

And this is why Angus Òg, the young God, is more ancient than the land, the sea and the sky, yet is forever young. The ancient three have a set time, but it is in the heart of Angus that Time and Eternity, eternal joy and eternal hope lie.

This romantic tale gives some idea of the attributes of Angus and shows the acknowledgement that other Gods give to him. It also shows several threefold patterns, which are important within Celtic mythology in general and in some Pagan religious practices in particular. Angus has Lordship over the land, sea and sky. He was there before they existed and he will be there long after they have gone. It is in the places where the edges of these three realms meet that Angus can be felt at his most powerful. Consider the triple spiral that decorates the large boulder at the entrance to Angus's house, Newgrange: the spirals dance in their movement through time, space and lifecycles, yet they dance around an unmoving and eternal centre. In that centre is Angus, the Ever-Young God.

There are various versions of the story about how Angus came to be master of Newgrange. A 12th Century version states it is the Dagda who lived in Newgrange and Angus tricked him out of Newgrange at Samhain. A later 15th C version tells how Angus tricked his mother's husband from Newgrange. Regardless of who owned Newgrange, the point is that Angus *tricked* them out of the place. The symbolism and metaphorical meanings in both stories are worth some thought and study – there has been a 'forgetting' of some of his older aspects, that of trickster amongst them. But even as Angus slept for a thousand years, humanity did not truly forget him. How could we? His breath was in our kisses and his joy danced in our veins as we felt the year turn to the sun.

The Song of Wandering Aengus – WB Yeats Folklore

The Song of Wandering Aengus was published in 1899, in Yeats's collection *The Wind Among the Reeds.* It tells one of the more well-known stories about Angus, that of the biter bitten. Angus dreamt of the most beautiful girl he had ever seen. He had this dream every night for a year, and Angus grew more and more despondent, pining away for his dream girl. After a year, the dreams stopped and he saw her no more. Angus became ill with his longing for the dream girl he had fallen in love with. He wasted away so much that his parents feared he would die and sent for a Druid healer. The Druid took one look at Angus and realised it was for the love of a woman that Angus sickened. He advised Boann, Angus's mother, to seek out this girl. In a nutshell, it took many seekers to track down the girl: Caer Ibormeith, daughter of Ethal Anbual of Connaught. In some sources, Caer is referred to as a Celtic Goddess of dreams, which makes her an interesting counterpart to Angus's Scottish aspect as a seller of dreams.

Once Angus had found Caer, her father, Ethal, was not inclined to give his daughter to Angus and he agreed to let Angus have Caer only if he could pick her out from her handmaidens. Angus readily agreed to this; and Ethal led him to a lake where 50 swans swam. Caer and her handmaidens were Sidhe who spent half the year in human shape and half the year in the shape of swans. Ethal thought that Angus would not be able to tell Caer from the rest of the swan maidens, but he was wrong. Not only did Angus identify Caer from the gold necklace she wore, he immediately transformed himself into a swan and the two flew above the lake, singing and swooping in the joy of their love, changing from swans to humans at Beltane and back to swans at Samhain.

This is a very much shortened version of the story of Angus Òg and one of his loves, Caer Ibormeith. The interesting aspect of the story is that, even for the Gods, love is not always easy. Angus pines whilst the search is made for the girl of his dreams. Once she is found, he does not give up when her father presents him with difficulties. He perseveres in his quest and he is willing to both transform himself for love and to be transformed by love. On one level, Yeats's Poem alludes to this sense of Angus wandering on his quest, of seeking something that is just glanced, just within reach. However, like many of Yeats's early poems, there are at least three levels within the poem and all of them have something to teach us in Pathworking.

The Poem

The Song of Wandering Aengus

I went out to the hazel wood,
Because a fire was in my head,
And cut and peeled a hazel wand,
And hooked a berry to a thread;
And when white moths were on the wing,
And moth-like stars were flickering out,
I dropped the berry in a stream
And caught a little silver trout.

When I had laid it on the floor
I went to blow the fire aflame,
But something rustled on the floor,
And some one called me by my name:
It had become a glimmering girl
With apple blossom in her hair
Who called me by my name and ran
And faded through the brightening air.

Though I am old with wandering
Through hollow lands and hilly lands,
I will find out where she has gone,
And kiss her lips and take her hands;
And walk among long dappled grass,
And pluck till time and times are done
The silver apples of the moon,
The golden apples of the sun.
WB Yeats (1899)

Commentary

Angus is disturbed by his own dreams and by the gifts of Bridget:
'a fire was in my head'. On its literal level, this gives an image of

a God with fire around his head, a picture which brings a sense of awe and wonder. Such an image is a timely reminder that although Angus is a gentle, quiet God, he is a God and as such, should be approached with due reverence. As a metaphor, it tells us that he is inspired; whether by passion, poetry or love is something to be explored.

A magical atmosphere is established in the first stanza with the repetition of *hazel*. Within Celtic mythology – and within many Pagan traditions – the hazel is a magical tree, symbolising wisdom, learning and knowledge. The tale of Connla's Well tells us that even the nuts of this tree are imbued with this magic. The hazel trees that grew over Connla's Well dropped nuts into the water: the trout that lived in the well ate these nuts and, as a result of this, people who ate the fish from the well were given the gifts of deep knowledge and wisdom.

The implication within 'I cut a peeled a hazel wand' is that Angus creates the magic to explore the inspiration that has hit him. Thus, he signifies he will use the wisdom of the tree to help him find an answer to the inspiration that has struck him. He then ties a 'berry to a thread' and begins fishing. A berry is the beginning of a new plant; it is the seed of generation. Its colour is generally red, a colour associated with love and passion. Even a short reflection on this image tells us this is a beginning. It is Angus's journey – a beginning for him. It is also a beginning for us, as we explore the Pathworking possibilities of the poem.

The poem is a dramatic monologue, spoken by the persona of Angus. There are eight syllables per line, which mimics the rhythm of a human heart beating at a faster rate than normal, given that iambic pentameter, which is ten beats per line, replicates the normal pace of a human heartbeat as the lungs fill. Therefore, Angus is excited by the fire in his head and aware that something is about to happen. He faces this by going to a place associated with wisdom in order to explore his feelings. The repetition of 'and' gives a tone of storytelling to the poem, we are being invited to listen as Angus relates this tale.

The importance of colours and their symbolism in this poem are emphasised by repetition: 'white' is the colour associated with Celtic Deities in their manifestations as animals. Indeed, white Otherworld animals often appear on the human plane, which is why sightings of white stags, magpies and so forth are considered special and treated as messengers from the Gods by those who know what and who the animals represent. There is an additional meaning to the use of white, when it is considered alongside the red of the berry: these are the colours of life, the male and female sides of fertility; but again, it is the beginning of fertility, the potential. Just as the berry contains the seeds of new life, new beginnings, so does the production of sperm and the fertility indicated by menstrual blood indicate the potential for fertility, for new beginnings and new life. This is further shown by the 'apple blossom' – the flowering of youth, of future possibilities. All is yet potential, awaiting fertilisation and growth.

Angus catches a 'silver trout', which has connotations of wisdom through the tale of the fish in Connla's Well. Silver is a colour with connotations of the night and of the moon, it is a colour associated with a Goddess. These ideas reflect upon Caer Ibormeith as a Celtic Goddess of dreams. Although the persona does not name the girl of his dreams (as Angus did not know it until he found her) the 'glimmering girl' names him. The importance of names needs no long explanation: magical practice and children's stories abound with examples of the power in the knowledge of names. She has his name and Angus is under her spell; he has fallen for her.

That she is a magical being, a member of the Sidhe, is inherent in both the onomatopoeia and alliteration in *glimmering girl*. Glimmering suggests an ethereal quality to her, as if she is made from light and shadow. In addition, the word sounds like it fades in and out, with a heavy stress on the first and last syllable and a lighter unstressed syllable in the middle. All of this tells us she is a woman of the Sidhe, one of the twilight people.

She turns away from him as dawn begins to break: 'faded through the brightening air', as do all dreams. Her power may be tied to the night, to the shadows or to the realms of dreams and magic. However, Angus will not allow this dream to fade away in sad echoes; he will find her, even though he is 'old with wandering'. The very beautiful declaration that he will find her 'through hollow lands and hilly lands' is not only a statement of how far he will travel to find her, but a statement about the landscape itself, the curves of a woman's body embodied in the rise and fall of the landscape. Anyone who has seen the Sleeping Beauty on the Isle of Lewis, or similar landscape features, can immediately identify with this imagery. It is loaded with sensuality, not only for the love between people, but also for the love of the land.

Yeats ends the poem by reminding us that Angus is the Ever-Young God, he will search till time and tide are done. He was conceived, gestated and born in a space outside of time when the moon and the sun stood still – time is an irrelevance for him, no matter how long it takes him he will find his dream girl. His resolution in following his dream is something from which we can draw strength.

Dream Angus – Traditional Scottish Lullaby
Folklore

In Scotland, Angus is the seller of dreams; it is he who brings sweet sleep – or nightmares. **Dream Angus** is sung as a lullaby to children[6] and the gentleness in the song promises these will be pleasant dreams. It has such a gentle rhythm and a simple, haunting melody; it is perfect for the purpose of lulling a child to sleep. However, like many a fragmentary piece of folklore and half-remembered customs, there are deeper truths and insights to be gained by closely looking at the lyrics.

Angus is the Guardian of the Dream Realm and it is he who

will keep children safe from the night terrors – or those ill-formed elementals that inhabit the liminal spaces, looking for a way into our world, whether through dreams or madness. Such creatures are the inhabitants of nightmares and those who would walk between the worlds should remember such dangers exist. Anyone who claims the realms are completely safe has probably not been there.

The song promises the child that Angus will bring them a dream, but this is much more than just a Scottish version of the Sandman legend, where sleep dust is sprinkled on the eyes of children. Angus is a major God and this old song, with its tinkers' refrain of 'dreams to sell' masks the beauty – and the simplicity – of honouring Angus.

The Poem/Lyrics
Dream Angus

Can ye no hush yer weepin?
A' the wee lambs are sleepin.
Birdies are nestling, nestling taegither
Dream Angus is hirplin oe'r the heather.

Dreams tae sell, fine dreams tae sell,
Angus is comin wi' dreams to sell.
Hush noo my bairny, sleep wioot fear,
Dream Angus will bring you a dream, my dear.

List tae the curlew cryin,
faint are the echoes dyin,
Even the birds an beasties are sleepin,
But my bonnie bairny's greetin, greetin.

Dreams tae sell, fine dreams tae sell,
Angus is comin wi' dreams to sell.
Hush noo my bairny, sleep wi oot fear,

Dream Angus will bring you a dream, my dear.

Soon the lavrock sings his song,
Welcomin in a braw new dawn.
Lambies coorie doon taegither,
Wi' the yowies in the heather.

Dreams tae sell, fine dreams tae sell,
Angus is comin wi' dreams to sell.
Hush noo my bairny, sleep wi oot fear,
Dream Angus will bring you a dream, my dear.
Traditional Scottish Lullaby

Commentary

The persona in the poem is a parent, soothing a fractious child to sleep by singing a lullaby. This is an age-old, cross-cultural human behaviour and one that is instantly recognisable, as are the associated feelings of comfort and calm, whether we place ourselves in the position of the child or the parent.

The lyrics begin with a plea to the child to quieten down. We can assume the child is a baby as they are the ones most likely to overtire themselves to the state where they fight sleep and their response is to cry with exhaustion. Given the belief in re-incarnation in Celtic mythology, babies are also the ones who have most recently re-entered into this realm and are just beginning their new dance on one arm of the spiral, having passed from life, through death and into re-birth. Perhaps some remnant of memory stays with a young baby, causing it to be afraid to sleep in case it returns to the place of re-birth. Perhaps these wakeful babies are those who will grow up to be naturally connected to the realms and to the Otherworld. Perhaps they are merely sleepless babies in need of soothing to sleep.

The gentleness of the request, juxtaposed with 'a the wee lambs are sleepin' is a way of distracting a child, making images of noises in the night disturbing the animals and not being welcomed by all who would rather be asleep. It conjures up the 2am wakefulness of a baby that all new parents know so well. The syllabic pattern echoes the calming influence of the words. The gradually lengthening syllables per line as the verse progresses– 8 /8 / 9 / 10 – mirrors the beat of the human heart, racing at first, then slowing to its normal beat, soothing the child and bringing it to a state of calm where sleep is possible.

The word choice 'hirplin' is interesting. It is Scots for limping and this is a strange reference to associate with Angus. In several pantheons the lame Gods are the master craftsmen, the ones who make the treasures of the Gods but are somehow apart from them as their lameness separates them from the other Gods. In one sense, applying this to Angus may be a reference to his crafting of dreams for sale, thus placing him firmly amongst the Craftspeople Gods. In another sense, it may merely be a reference to the awkwardness of moving across a wild, hilly, heather-covered landscape, again painting a picture for a child of the landscape it inhabits.

The repeated refrain 'Dreams to sell, fine dreams to sell' sounds like that of a tinker or pedlar approaching an outlying village. In times past, such visits from pedlars and tinkers would have been an event looked forward to by isolated villagers. The tinker would offer to mend old pots and pans and in his pack he would have had his goods for sale, the necessities and the small luxuries that make life pleasant. The pedlar may have carried even more exotic goods for sale. This metonymy defines Angus in this role: he is an itinerant traveller and a hawker of dreams.

This Angus sells dreams: this implies there is a price to pay. What this price may be will be explored later.

The sounds within the poem create a melancholy tone, as anyone who has heard a curlew singing and calling across the water's edge at twilight will testify. It can be an eerie, lonesome sound, which catches people off-guard when they do not know what it is. The symbolism of a bird that is at home in the three realms is important: this bird is an Otherworld bird singing in the new day as twilight falls. The sad echoes of its song invite reflection upon things half-forgotten and, in that sense, it is not surprising that the curlew has long been associated with sorrow. The sorrows of being half-forgotten belong to the Sidhe, who have been diminished in importance through time. The curlew is also associated with the west, particularly in Yeats's poetry; and in this sense, they can be seen as a link between the ancestors and the living as the lands and Otherworld realms of the Sidhe were held to be in the west.

The child is re-assured and sleep comes. Angus will bring the child sweet dreams. The thrice-repeated chorus reminds us that we pay to dream and to sleep without fear; Angus will protect us in our dreams. But what price could a small child possibly offer a God? The answer is simple: the price is memory and metonymy. By singing this aspect of Angus, a parent teaches a child that Angus is a gentle God who will bless their dreams and protect them from nightmares. As they grow, children will make connections with the land, their ancestors and – through Angus – the realms of dreams and the Otherworld. The remembrance of the old ones is the price for all to pay: the stories carried in their blood and bone, the stories of their ancestors and the stories of their land, their waters and their skies. From those who do remember all these things emerge those people who would adore and walk the path of Angus, thus bringing the Gods back into this world. The adoration of Angus is simple, yet those who develop it, who answer Angus' call, can find even simplicity is not always straightforward.

To remember and to see Angus in the land, in the sea and in the sky – that is the price. That is the tinker's bargain.

Pathworking
Acknowledging Angus

Should you wish to acknowledge Angus, try meditating in a place where the land, sea and sky meet. In choosing such a place, you are respecting the old Gods of Scotland and Ireland – and older than those is Angus. He is on the edges – he holds the keys to the realms. Offer what seems right. He may come to you in the form of a bird, he may come to you in dreams, or he may come to you in feelings of sheer joy and life pulsing through you. You will know when you are Angus blessed.

Those fortunate enough to receive training and guidance from Pagan Elders who knew Angus were sometimes asked to contemplate a question in order to help them discover the first steps on their individual path. The question posed was: 'Which is stronger, stone or water?' There is no right answer to this, only the answer that is right for an individual. The question was considered for a few months, followed by a meditation into a trance state where a personal answer was given. This was not a task to rush through in order to move on to the next thing. The time spent in thinking about the question allowed the Gods to measure the seekers' mettle; to see those qualities within the seeker that the Gods may choose to work with. It allowed the Gods to assess who the seeker was and what they may become. For those who would follow Angus as their major God , the answer was water.

Why is Angus water? Water flows. It penetrates. It cleanses. Water guards the entrances to the Otherworld and water has properties that mirror land, sea and sky: solid, liquid and gas. Water will overcome stone. Water can bless and water can destroy. Humans cannot live without water. Water has many moods. Water is a changing emotion. Water just *is*. And water remains water, even as it mimics the land, the sea and the sky by being solid, liquid and gas. At its centre it is still water. As Angus is at the centre of the triple spiral as it dances through its changing meanings, he remains Angus. These are the reasons that water is Angus.

Paganism is experiential and personal and this applies no matter how long or how short a time a path has been walked. Listening to and experiencing Gods and Goddesses takes practice, particularly if the seeker comes from a background where others were invested with the power to intercede between Deity and follower. This is not to say there is nothing to learn from more experienced Pagan Elders; these Elders are the ones who have the knowledge to guide you as you find your personal path.

Choose a place by flowing water at twilight, where you will not be disturbed. Ask permission of the Guardians of the place to Pathwork and make libations to them. When you have received permission, create a small circle around yourself to prevent any unwanted visitors from whichever realms realise a portal has opened between the worlds.

Sit by the water and watch the light dance over the surface. Look in the direction the water flows and allow your mind to empty. Breathe slowly and deeply, all the while watching the dancing water. Feel the urgency of the dream of Angus portrayed in Yeats's poem and marry it with your own desire to know him. Hear the refrain of the lullaby faintly echoing around your head. Know your dreams and through them, know Angus. Be honest in your intent and your willingness to pay the price. Then allow the water to tell you a story of long ago and of now:

'Leave that, sit a while with me, here by the fire. We're both too old and too ancient to be fussing overmuch with pots and pans,' said the young man, as he stared into the fire.

His companion laughed. 'To be sure, we're both too old to be worrying about tidying our halls!' Her tinkling laughter followed her graceful movements, as she joined him. They both stared into the fire awhile, lost in aeons of memory. Then the young man spoke.

'Do you remember the days when our names were on all lips, when we walked the earth – the days when people worshipped us?'

'Indeed I do, Angus Òg, indeed I do. And there was no finer or sweeter music than that from your harp, for it made all who heard it happy in their hearts. Yours was the breath of love and the joy of living.'

'As yours was the joys of hearth and home, of children, Brigit, remember?'

Brigit said nothing but her eyes shone. He watched her face, saw the longing for past glories dance from her eyes. Then she said,

'We can go back there. Nothing is ever really forgotten. Shall I tell you your tales again? Of the stories they still tell in the lands where we danced, where we loved and were loved?'

Angus put some more wood on the fire; stretched out comfortably and answered her. 'Please do.' A sigh of pleasure ended his words. Overhead, four white birds circled the pair by the fire, then landed beside Angus Òg, fully intent on hearing Brigit's tales.

Angus smiled at them; these birds had been his companions and faithful servants for centuries. No matter how wide across the world he sent them on errands, they always came happily home to him, singing as sweetly as the day they first wooed their mates.

'I'll start at the beginning,' she said. 'How we made this world.'

Angus wiggled his toes in the warmth from the fire and sat back, all the more ready to listen.

As the tales are told, listen. Listen to the words and to the silences. You will know when it is time to leave; there are only so many things a little human can take in at once. But come back slowly, very slowly. You have been in the company of two very powerful beings, who, whilst not directly acknowledging you, are more than aware you are there. How could it be otherwise? You are there at their implicit invitation and the stories they tell are for your benefit. If you are serious in your intent, this campfire is an easy place to return to, an eternal now that links the past, the present and the future. In short, the centre of the triple spiral, whose heart is Angus Òg.

Part 2: Ritual to Welcome Angus and Bride

Writing ritual is an honour – and a way of honouring our Gods. Each of us has our own preferred method of writing and our own preferred times of celebrations. The following is not a didactic attempt to layout a ritual, it is merely offered as an outlined example of a rite to celebrate the sacred marriage at Beltane. The original was more in depth and written specifically for an established group.

Welcome Home to the King of Summer

The focus of this ritual is to welcome Angus's return from the Green Isle in the West and to celebrate his marriage with Bride. Their marriage celebrates the coming of summer and the time of peace and plenty. The Cailleach has been defeated and she has gone to the Isle of Youth, to drink from the well of the young. She is a maiden again and winter will not return until she ages.

The intent of the ritual is to remove any personal negativity that has built up since Samhain and welcome the sun into our lives.

This rite will take place where the liminal space is strongest – where the land, sea and sky meet. The preparation work is to meditate, holding a stone. All the negativity of life since Samhain is to be focused within the stone. The stone will be cast into the sea – the troubles and negativity are symbolically washed away, cleansing the turn of the year and blessing the new beginning of Beltane.

Cast circle, sing in land, sea and sky. Libations.

Speaker 1:
Beira is the Cailleach, the crone Goddess of Winter. It is she who washes her cloak in the Corryvrecken whirlpool in the Sound of Jura and spreads it out on the hills to dry. It is she who causes snow to cover the land. Storms and winds accompany her reign.

Speaker 2:

It is she who causes Angus Òg to live on the Green Isle of the West, the Land of Youth.

Speaker 3:

But it was Angus himself, the seller of dreams, who first saw Bride in a dream and he fell in love with her. In his dream, he spoke to an old man and asked why Bride wept. 'She weeps because she is the prisoner of the Cailleach, and Beira treats her cruelly.'

Speaker 2:

Angus wanted to set off to Scotland to rescue Bride, but the King of the Green Isle said:

Speaker 3:

'It is the wolf-month. Do not trust the temper of the wolf.'

Speaker 1:

Angus answered: 'I shall borrow for February three glorious days from August.'

Speaker 2:

He did this and the ocean slept gently and the sun shone. Angus mounted his white horse and rode eastwards to Scotland, crossing the Minch and reaching the Grampians as dawn broke. Up and down the land Angus rode, but he could not find Bride anywhere. Yet spring stirred in the February sun.

Speaker 3:

Bride too, stirred and her dreams told her that Angus searched for her.

Speaker 1:

Beira was angered that Angus sought to free Bride and on the third evening of his visit, she raised a great storm that blew Angus back to the Green Isle. But he returned – and each time he returned, Beira again raised a storm that blew him back to the Island.

Speaker 2:

But Angus persevered and he rescued Bride from the clutches of the Cailleach.

Speaker 3:

Life is a circle and all things have a beginning, an end and a beginning again. All things love, die and are re-born. Beira is the Cailleach. Praise the Cailleach in her time and season. Praise her return to the Land of Youth.

Speaker 1:

Beira was angered when she knew that Angus had found Bride. She raised her magic hammer and smote the earth until it had frozen solid again. Yet the birds still sang of the marriage of Angus and Bride and she knew her reign was at an end.

Speaker 2:

And at Beltane, Angus and Bride were joined in the sacred marriage.

Speaker 3:

The people sang with joy and the shepherds declared that summer had properly come. Bride and Angus walked over the land. She waved her hands, weaving her magic and Angus sang his spells, weaving his magic – and the land grew green and beautiful. All the people in Scotland felt their presence in the land and their hearts were filled with joy and hope.

Speaker 1:
So Angus begins his reign as King of Summer, with Bride at his side, as his queen. May his laughter sound out across Scotland and may this land and its people burst forth in fruitfulness and joy.

Praise Summer
Gather love,
Listen for their names
Sung on the wind
Laughing across the land,
Dancing across the water,
Blessing the crops
Who flourish, waiting
For the call of Lughnasadah.

Speaker 2:
Welcome home to the King of Summer

All:
Welcome Angus and Bride.
(*Libations made.*)

Speaker 1:
It is a time of new beginnings and new hope. Much will have happened to us since Samhain. We have banished our negativity and the things we need to release and placed them in these stones.

Manannan Mac Lir, we ask your kindness in taking them from us.

(*Throw stones into the sea – a waning moon and an out-going tide are best.*)

We offer this libation in thanks.

(*Pour beer for the Old man.*)

Praise the three ancient ones

Gather love,
Listen to their names

Sung on the wind
Laughing across the land,
Dancing across the water:

Manannan, Aesus, Keithor,
And bless these three
Who flourish, waiting
In the service of Bride,
And of Angus,
The most ancient of them all.
Yet always the ever young.
Libations, sing out land, sea and sky. Uncast circle.

Part 3: Visions

Transformation: Ways of Seeing

One of the joys of exploring poetry as Pathworking is the realisation that we think with the heart as well as the head. When we follow this through, we accept that this dual thinking somehow gives us more understanding, which can be a mixed blessing. Sometimes, to understand fully, we have to let go of old habits and old beliefs. This is never easy. For some people, the path of least resistance is their chosen one and looking at the world through the lens of an 'other' is easier than forging a path of their own. There is no fault in this – it is how the world works. However, those who would define their own path need to go through this process of letting go and realigning their own thoughts in balance with their own personal feelings and experiences. The next two poems explore this letting go and look at what may have been given in its place.

The Collar-Bone of a Hare – WB Yeats

Yeats wrote this poem in 1915, when he was in his fiftieth year. This is a time when many of us realise that it is likely there are more years behind us than lie ahead; and consequently, we take stock. It would seem to have been so for Yeats.

The woman who was the passion and inspiration in Yeats's life was Maud Gonne, an ardent fighter in the cause of Irish Nationalism. They met in the late 1880s and, for Yeats, Gonne was his passion, his inspiration and his torment. He proposed to her on at least four occasions over the years, but she turned him down every time. His refusal to share her politics was a bone of contention between them: Yeats sought an Irish identity within the media of the arts; she preferred a more direct approach. Such a combination of ideas would make for an uneasy breakfast companion and it could be said that Gonne was clear-headed enough to foresee such a union would not work when their ideas were so different. Instead, Gonne chose to marry Major John MacBride in 1903. He was a soldier and an Irish freedom fighter. Their marriage did not last, although they had a son. By 1904, they were separated. MacBride's role in the fight for Irish liberation led to him becoming involved in the 1916 Easter Uprising and he was executed by the British for his part in it.

That Yeats was jealous and bitter about Gonne's marriage to MacBride is evident in some of his poems from this time. Not only had his great passion and inspiration been taken from him by another man; that man was a Roman Catholic as well. Yeats disliked Irish Catholicism and Gonne had previously converted to this faith, before her marriage to MacBride. However, differences aside, Gonne continued her friendship with Yeats and they finally slept together in 1908. Yeats must have felt he was reaching the woman of his dreams at last, but for Gonne the night was an episode not to be repeated. One can only imagine how Yeats felt about this. It is hard not to feel sorry for him and to understand a personal level of sadness in a line from a later poem, *Easter 1916*: 'too long a sacrifice makes a stone of the heart.'

However, to return to 1915, Yeats appears to have been appraising his life and he seems to have yearned for a wife, and perhaps children. His considerations of things led him to see his situation clearly and the consideration of how things are viewed is at the heart of his poem. There is much to be learned about vision and ways of seeing from his musings in *The Collar-Bone of a Hare.*

Folklore

The symbolism and significance of the hare within both Scottish and Irish folklore is well documented. Even the Romans commented on the taboo the Celts had about eating the hare – and the faint echo of this taboo exists still. To do so was considered to be akin to eating your grandmother. This folk belief picks up on the idea of the hare as a sacred animal, one who is associated with the crone/the winter Goddess of Ireland and Scotland, the Cailleach – and by extension, with the ancestors. The hare is an Otherworld animal, sometimes she is a messenger of the Goddess, and sometimes she is a transformation of the Goddess herself. Folklore is full of stories about people who wound hares, only to find later that some old woman in their village has an injury corresponding to the one inflicted on the animal. Tinkers' stories use the hare as a symbol of fertility, long life and re-birth, in other words, of the cycle of life, death and re-incarnation, which ties in with the story already related about the Cailleach, Angus and Bride and their dance through the seasons of the year. Tales expand in the telling and no doubt stories about hares grew in stature and importance as they were re-told in villages and by itinerants on their journeys through Scotland and Ireland.

It is easy to see from the folk belief about 'eating your own grandmother' why the hare is associated with the Cailleach, the crone Goddess, who undergoes her own yearly transformation from old crone to young woman and back again. The shape-shifting abilities of the Goddess/hare are bestowed upon the village crones of folklore. However, they are also associated with the Sidhe, as animals that leap the boundaries between here and the Otherworld. There are many superstitions naming unspec-ified, but dreadful, consequences should they be deliberately harmed. This, however, does not seem to have prevented the protagonist of many a folk story from wounding a hare he believed to be a witch in another form. In general, the stories do not relate what the punishment was on the person who hurt the hare, only their smug satisfaction at exposing a witch amongst them. In a sense, half the story is untold – the insult to the

Goddess should not remain unpunished, but the story ends where the propaganda begins. By this I mean that the 'new' religious beliefs of Christianity were in the ascendancy at the time these tales were collected and written down. Perhaps the exposure of the old woman who is discovered as a witch; and who could shape-shift into a hare, has become the new focus of the story. Perhaps the old point of the story was to admonish people who forgot the rules of ancient Celtic hospitality and looking after your own. Why else would an old woman need to transform into a hare in order to eat?

The most famous case of a witch who claimed to be able transform into a hare in Scotland is that of Isobel Gowdie. Her story is a remarkable account of transforming corn stalks into horses; taking part in wild hunts and blasting those below with elf bolts. There are further accounts of changing into animals such as cats, crows and hares. Gowdie would seem to have had a preference for being a hare and there are several accounts of her shape-shifting to enable her to come and go undetected. She was also – according to some accounts – a friend of Jean Gordon, the niece of Robert Gordon of Gordonstoun. He was a nobleman widely believed to be a wizard.

It is unclear what prompted Gowdie to confess, especially in an era when this was signing her own death warrant. She was arrested on April 12th 1664 and between 13th April and May 27th 1662, made her four confessions. These confessions resulted in another 40 people from Auldearn being sent to trial as witches.

Gowdie's trial was heard by the Privy Council in May 1662.[7] The records are not complete and it is not recorded what the outcome of the trial was. However, it is unlikely that she – or the 40 other souls tried as a result of her confessions – would have escaped execution. It is likely that Isobel Gowdie met her death by strangling, followed by burning, on Gallows Hill, just outside Auldearn, Nairnshire.

Moreover, as well as the tales of hares in folklore and in the confessions of witches, there are other tantalising references to hares – almost like a half-remembered dream that can't quite be grasped. The national flower of Scotland is the thistle, but another flower closely associated with the country is the bluebell. The Scottish bluebell is not the wild hyacinth-like plant known as a bluebell in other parts of the UK, it is the flower also called a harebell. This may seem like a tenuous link to folklore about hares, but the Scottish bluebell is believed to have medicinal properties, allegedly being good for strengthening the heart and the lungs. The juice of the flowers is reputed to help witches transform into hares and the roots also contain properties necessary to make flying ointment.

This is just a very short exploration of some of the folklore and beliefs about hares, but it is enough to emphasise the importance of the animal and its links to the Goddess. It is an animal associated with the feminine, with boundaries and with transformation.

An Dà Shealladh is Scots Gaelic for second sight. Sometimes those who have this ability are also able to remotely view events at a distance. Those who had the gift of second sight often considered it a curse and both folklore and written sources are full of tales of those who thought that way about it. There are several stories in which the Good Folk have endowed this gift on a human who has been helpful to them in some way. Other stories tell of women who have been taken to act as nursemaid to a Sidhe child and who break their enchanted imprisonment by splashing something into their eye. Not only does this allow them to see the realm of the Sidhe clearly, it enables them to escape. In these stories, it is not uncommon for the Sidhe to blind the woman before her return to this realm, claiming this was not a gift that was freely given.

Arguably, the most famous seer in Scots folklore is the Brahan Seer, Kenneth Mackenzie, (*Coinneach Odhar*). He was famed for both his gift of prophecy and for his ability to view at a distance.

He was given a seeing stone by a gypsy woman, or a corpse returning to its grave, depending on which story you read. A seeing stone is a stone with a hole in it and it was this that aided his second sight. Another name for these seeing stones is a hagstone, which reflects an association with the Cailleach, the old hag of winter.

However, sadly for Kenneth, his ability to see led to his execution for witchcraft. He was asked by the Countess of Seaforth to use his stone and tell her how her husband's business in Paris was progressing. MacKenzie duly did so, to discover the 'business' the Count was involved with included a rather glamorous Frenchwoman. He obfuscated initially, but the Countess forced the truth from him. The Countess of Seaforth was so enraged by this news, she ordered MacKenzie arrested. In a classic case of shooting the messenger, he was then burnt to death in a tar barrel at Chanonry Point, Fortrose. There is still a memorial to him at the spot he was killed. His crime was to see what was really there – and to speak of it to one who didn't want to hear the truth.

Seeing what is really there, taking stock of the present and seeing the likely future were all things that concerned Yeats on a very personal level in 1915. However, there is more than Yeats's personal anguish in this poem. It is a poem that explores transformations and ways of seeing that speaks to us all.

Poem

The Collar-Bone of a Hare

Would I could cast a sail upon the water
Where many a king has gone
And many a king's daughter,
And alight at the comely trees and the lawn,
The playing upon pipes and the dancing,
And learn that the best thing is

To change my loves while dancing
And pay but a kiss for a kiss.

I would find by the edge of that water
The collar-bone of a hare
Worn thin by the lapping of water,
And pierce it through with a gimlet, and stare
At the old bitter world where they marry in churches,
And laugh over the untroubled water
At all who marry in churches,
Through the thin white bone of a hare.
WB Yeats (1915)

Commentary

This poem was written at a crux in Yeats' life. He contemplates
the veracity of his life's path; and what love has been for him, in
a profound manner that must have caused him some anguish.
His hesitant: 'Would I could' indicates his uncertainty and his
wish to be free of the games he may have felt Maud Gonne
played with his feelings for her. He wishes to enter the realms of
the Sidhe, but whether this is as a visitor or on his last journey is
not clear. The ambivalence of 'cast a sail upon the water/where
many a king has gone' does suggest the final journey to the west.
Yeats longs for the delights of the Otherworld, dancing to fairy
pipes on a verdant ground. He is aware that his lack of a wife is
a sorrow for him and he knows that the remedy is in his own
hands. He has realised that Maud Gonne will never be his, even
though she was long-separated from MacBride by 1915. The sad,
bitter-sweet tone of his expressed wish 'And learn that the best
thing is/to change my loves while dancing/and pay but a kiss for
a kiss' shows his realisation that the love he feels for Gonne is
one-sided and, should he ever succeed in his quest for a family
life, he must let go of this love for her. Indeed, the recognition
that love should be balanced is indicated in the lines 'pay but a

kiss for a kiss'. Perhaps Yeats realised that there was no balance in his relationship with Gonne, he saw one thing, she another.

That Yeats yearns for clarity of vision is evident in his use of the metaphor of a holed bone to 'see' through. Such a metaphor taps into well-established folklore about second sight. Yeats then develops this further by stating he would find not a seeing stone, but a thinned hare bone by the water's edge. He places this magical item in a place where the edges of land, sea and sky meet, indicating that this bone is a gift from the Gods. The symbolism of the hare, as discussed, represents fertility, the Goddess and life cycles. Ancestral memory is carried in the blood and bone of animals; therefore the significance of using the hare bone – which carries not only the animal's heredity but the magical and folklore heredity of this sacred animal – cannot be overlooked. Yeats is appealing to the Goddess to help him see clearly in respect of matters relating to his life. It could be argued that Yeats is not quite ready to let go of his love for Gonne and that he realises he must make himself alter his thinking. Usually the gift of a seeing stone is one that is stumbled upon, the stone with a hole worn through it naturally by wind and weather. Yeats takes himself outside of his ordinary life, to a place where he is on the outside looking in at his life. He stands on the shores of the Otherworld, holding the bone he would 'pierce (...) through with a gimlet'. The word choices of *pierce* and *gimlet* are forceful. To pierce something is to deliberately force it and a gimlet is a sharp tool used to make small holes through tough materials. The imagery created here is one of force, both physically, as Yeats prepares the hare bone, and metaphorically, as he realises the answers to his yearnings are in his own hands.

Once he has created his seeing bone, Yeats stands himself in the Otherworld, staring back across smooth waters, seeing what is really there rather than what he had perceived when standing in this realm, looking across stormy waters to the Otherworld. The symbolism of the water is obvious, his troubles are in this realm and he needs to stand on the shores of the Otherworld, where there are no troubles and look across their smooth waters in order to see his life clearly.

His summary of his view from the Otherworld is contained in the word *laugh* and at the repetition of 'marry in churches'. That this is aimed at the conventions of his time is obvious, as is its probable swipe at Maud Gonne's marriage to MacBride. Although she had been separated from her husband since 1904, her divorce petition had been denied and technically, Gonne was still MacBride's wife. There is an unpleasant tone of bitterness in this – Gonne had previously had two children with Lucien Millevoye, her married French lover. Her son did not survive, but her daughter – Iseult – did. For the early part of her life, Iseult was passed off in Irish public life as Gonne's niece, instead of her daughter, in deference to the mores surrounding illegitimate children in that era.

That Gonne had then married and been denied a divorce was ironic for a woman who had been unconventional enough to have two children by a previous lover. Yeats's laughter at 'those who marry in churches' may be part ironic, part manic as he realises that, whilst she may have been his muse, his passion and his inspiration, these feelings were not equally reciprocated. Balance in a relationship is one where each partner 'pay but a kiss for a kiss'. He may have come to the conclusion that Gonne, too, had been fooled by love, given she had a married lover and a husband from whom she parted after a year or so of marriage. His laughter at the irony in a system that allowed couples to separate but not divorce was evident in his years as a senator. He spoke out against the Catholic Church's opposition to divorce and the position of people who found themselves in a hinterland when marriages broke down and re-marriage was not possible as divorce was anathema to the church.

This poem points to a change in Yeats and his feelings for Gonne. He knew he wanted a family life and he came to realise that this would never be with Gonne. Although she remained important to him, he began the slow process of accepting the reality of his relationship with Gonne. He realised that if he was to have a wife, it would have to be another woman, not Maud Gonne. 1916 -17 were busy years for Yeats, as he determinedly went about making his clarity of vision a reality. He proposed to 25-year-old Georgie Hyde Lees and they married in October 1917. The couple went on to have two children.

The Collar-Bone of a Hare focuses on a transition point in Yeats's life and his need for a deep, fundamental shift in the way he thought. It is this aspect that we can Pathwork – the seeing what is really there, letting go of the illusions and the acceptance of change being something we can choose to address, no matter how painful. Before exploring how this poem could be used for Pathworking, it is useful to juxtapose it with Seumas O'Sullivan's poem *Credo.*

Credo

Seumus O'Sullivan (James Sullivan Starkey 1879-1958) was the editor of *The Dublin Magazine* and, as a poet and a writer; he was also a part of the Irish Literary Revival Movement. This movement aimed to give voice to what it meant to be Irish; to find an Irish identity through the exploration of Ireland's ancient history and stories and to define who the Irish were without reference to the cultural values of Britain. It arose as a literary movement, at a time of great political upheaval and uncertainty; and it fed in to Irish political and cultural life. O'Sullivan was part of this vibrant cultural life, alongside such other luminaries as Synge, Yeats and AE Russell.

Credo was published in a collection of poems entitled: *An Epilogue to the Praise of Angus* in 1914. It is a poem which perhaps some might consider belongs at the beginning of a Pathworking, but it is also a poem which ties in with Yeats's *The Collar-Bone of a Hare*. O'Sullivan's poem explores the ability to see things clearly; to stand apart from them and really look; and it explores the realisation that the religion we may have grown up with no longer fulfils our spiritual needs. It is this latter sense of the realisation that our childhood beliefs do not fulfil our needs which suggests the poem belongs to the beginning of Pathworking – a meditation on a personal *Credo*. However, it is the former sense that complements Yeats – O'Sullivan's poem looks into the vision to see what is really there.

The title itself reflects the Christianity of Ireland in O'Sullivan's time; it is the Christian profession of faith and belief. Roman Catholicism was the religion of the majority of the Irish population in O'Sullivan's time. It is not within the scope of this book to look at the background politics of late 19th Century/early 20th Century Ireland: suffice to say there were tensions within political, social and cultural life that would eventually lead to war and the Partition of Ireland. Imagine O'Sullivan on his own quest for the Divine, in the midst of this.

O'Sullivan was rightly proud of his family's involvement with Methodism and in the fact that his ancestors lived the faith they professed. However, O'Sullivan seems not to have been able to find his own spirituality in Methodism, and to have felt that it had nothing to say that made his soul sing. Indeed, he found the interminable Sunday services – of which he was expected to attend several on the Sabbath – an ordeal. His interest in other ways of finding Deity led him to explore other churches and other kinds of faiths. Again, he does not seem to have found what he sought in any building, as his poem *Credo* makes clear.

The Poem

Credo

I cannot pray, as Christians use to pray,
Before the holy Rood,
Nor on the sacred mysteries seven, as they,

Believing brood.

Nor can I say with those whom pride makes sure,
Our hearts emancipate
Have scorn of ancient symbols that endure
Out-lasting late.

For I have seen Lord Angus in the trees.
And bowing heard
When Spring a lover whispered in their leaves
The living word.

Have known the sun, the wind's sweet agency,
And the soft rains that bless,
And lead the year through coloured pageantry,
To fruitfulness.

Yea, by the outstretched hands, the dimming sight,
The pierced side,
Know when in every bough that shrinks from light,
The Lord of life has died.
O'Sullivan (1914)

Commentary

Credo is Latin for 'I Believe' and it was a prayer recited in Latin during certain Catholic rituals and as part of the mass service. The *Credo* was often sung, perhaps echoing older traditions where singing in the Gods to a rite was commonplace. The *Credo* was taught to children, who learned it by rote; and who probably never gave it an analytical thought when they grew to adulthood. Therefore, O'Sullivan starts his poem with a title familiar to both Irish Catholics and to other denominations of Christians at that time: a simple statement of faith: 'I Believe'.

However, O'Sullivan's poem is a personal statement of belief, born from analysing his own beliefs as an adult, not merely a functional reiteration of accepted dogma. In one sense, the poem could be read as a blasphemy, and no doubt still would be by some, but it is not. It is a beautiful, honest exploration of one man's personal interaction with Deity, his thoughts, his feelings and his conclusions. This poem is visionary and at its heart is the ability to see things clearly and honestly.

O'Sullivan has doubts about those who say amen to the *Credo* of Christianity. He does not understand praying in this sense, nor how connection can be made with the Divine in a religion that originated in other lands. What O'Sullivan believes appears indigenous and to be older – much older – than Catholicism or the other Christianities in Ireland.

His first line negates the *Credo*: '*I cannot pray*'. It is almost a lament, as if he has a problem tearing at his soul. Contemplation of the poem reveals the nature of this problem as he continues: '*as Christians use to pray*'. A superfluous attention to the words may lead the reader to substitute 'used to' for 'use to' and the power of his phrase is lost. Attention to – and reflection upon – the word choice 'use' reveals a different thought process. The small verb 'use' has many meanings: 'to make use of', 'to put into service' and 'to take unfair advantage' being but three. O'Sullivan says he cannot make use of Christian prayer, nor put into service all that he was taught as a child. The word is written in the present tense – this is the point of the poem. Christian prayer has no meaning for him; he cannot use it to connect spiritually.

The 'holy Rood' is the wooden screen, often with a crucifix on it, which separated the people from the priest, which was a common feature of old chapels and churches. The lack of capitalisation on *holy* emphasises the lack of connection to Deity O'Sullivan feels. He feels there is nothing sacred about a mechanism whose function is to separate the people from their God. He sees no need for either the screen or the priest or minister to stand between him and his Gods – his interaction is not one of separation or intercession, but of unity. An older meaning of the word 'rood' is a 'measure of land' – the connotations of 'measure' imply a niggardly apportioning of a resource that once belonged to all communally. Perhaps this is how O'Sullivan saw the priest's role; hidden as he was behind the rood, separate from his congregation, doling out small portions of spirituality to his flock.

The rood was made of wood, usually intricately carved. But the wood is dead – it has been cut down, seasoned and used as a material to build the interior of the chapel. It no longer has any connection with the living, breathing forest. Instead of being a symbol of life, out in the open where all can see it rooted in the earth and reaching to the heavens, the tree has become the rood, a screen; a symbol of hidden things and a separation of humans from the Divine. A contemplation of the symbolism of the priest hiding behind this dead screen can be a rewarding exercise for those meditating on their own position with regards to the religion of their youth.

O'Sullivan's contemplation on beliefs continues with his bald statement that the 'sacred mysteries seven' hold no meaning for him. For the majority population in O'Sullivan's time, these refer to the sacraments of baptism, communion, confirmation, confession, marriage, holy orders and the last rites. The Catholic Church bestowed these sacraments on its flock – and again, the priests were the intermediaries between the believer and his Deity. O'Sullivan dismisses those who do believe in the almost contemptuous term: 'believing brood'. The alliteration echoes the sound of contempt, a strong indication of his thoughts on the 'brood' who worship these sacraments, despite the likelihood of only being able to avail themselves of six out of the seven in their lives. Ordination into the Catholic priesthood is the preserve of a male elite, not a shared sacrament available to all. Although women can take 'holy orders' in the sense of becoming nuns, they are not equal to priests nor do they hold powerful positions within the church as bishops, cardinals or popes. Perhaps this inequality was an additional part of what offended O'Sullivan about the church and he cannot understand why these things are not questioned by congregations. His feelings towards the people who attend services can be deducted from 'believing brood'. Brood has many meanings: it is the young offspring of a species. In this sense, O'Sullivan comments on the religion itself – an offshoot of Judaism that has both supplanted its parent and the indigenous religions of other countries. In comparison with both, it is a new religious movement, nowhere near as old as those it seeks to replace. The word also means 'to hatch' and in another sense, the connotations of 'hatching a plot' would be apposite – the historical plotting of the newcomer religion to rid itself of dissenters and heresies. Lastly, the word means 'to ponder' – and this is certainly what O'Sullivan is doing in respect of the concept of Credo.

This pondering leads him to regard the church's position in respect of older symbols. He cannot 'say with those whom pride makes sure' – he is not able to be as certain as the church or its believers that he would disdain older teachings. He is aware that pride comes before a fall and will not 'scorn ... ancient symbols that endure outlasting late'. Scotland and Ireland are full of carvings of 'ancient symbols outlasting late' – symbols much, much older than those of the relative late-comer of Christianity. These older symbols have meaning and they have survived through time.

O'Sullivan then states the reason he is at odds with the teachings of Christianity: 'For I have seen Lord Angus in the trees'. As already discussed, mythology tells stories of Angus as Lord of the realms of the land, sea and sky and the story related, about how the three ancient Gods were unable to wake him to bless the earth, emphasises his importance as a Deity of the living world. Angus is a living, breathing God and O'Sullivan knows him as such in his reverent act: 'And bowing heard'. His act of worship towards Angus is an experiential, direct inter-action with Deity, at odds with his experiences in churches. The knowledge of the natural life cycle of the seasons and Angus' role in it is emphasised as: 'The living word'. Although this is a title which is a play on the biblical quotation: 'for the word of God is living and effective'[8], used as a metaphor for the Christian Christ, O'Sullivan uses it as an image to show the living and effective blessings on the land by Angus: 'lead the year through coloured pageantry/to fruitfulness'. This is a powerful image. *Fruitfulness* is not only used in its literal sense in the cycle of life, but it also has connotations of metaphorical growth. In this case, it would seem that it is O'Sullivan's personal spiritual path that has borne fruit. He knows the Old Gods are not dead, but merely dormant and still accessible to those who would seek them. He sees them 'living and effective' in the green world around him.

However, O'Sullivan ends with a bitter comment on the thrall the Catholic Church held over Ireland by referring to the image of the crucified Christ, stretched over a cross made from dead wood. His final line: 'the Lord of life has died' may be read by Christians as a sad comment on the cruelty of the crucifixion. In the context of O'Sullivan's poem, it can be read as a comment on the diminishing of the Old Ones: the worship and reverence humankind once had for the trees, for rivers, for the living landscape have all been supplanted by a religion whose focus of worship is a dying man/God nailed to a dead piece of wood. For O'Sullivan, this man/God is one who has nothing to say directly to those who would follow him, all is said through the interme-diaries who construct elaborate rituals and rites which emphasise the power of the priests.

The early history of the church in Ireland is fascinating and beyond the scope of this text. However, suffice to say that the early Irish Church operated very differently from that of Rome. Many beliefs about Holy Places were absorbed, as were practices such as the giving of a christening piece to a child of the opposite sex from the newborn as the christening party left the house to have the baby baptised. The piece consisted of the first slice of the christening cake and a silver coin, given as a small gift in honour of God, to bless the baby and to give thanks for a safe delivery. It was important that the piece was given before the child was baptised – it was also an appeasement to the Good Neighbours of folklore. Even at a time when the child was to be introduced to a different God, the Sidhe and the old ways were put before the Christian God, even if the symbolism behind giving the piece had been forgotten. It was enough that it had to be done to bring good luck to the baby.

The practice of the christening piece is still extant in the Irish Catholic communities of Scotland and Ireland. In addition, it is pleasing to note this practice being brought back – as a blessing piece – in Pagan baby naming ceremonies.

However, as the *Tuatha De Danaan* faded into the hills, the experiential, personal nature of man's interaction with them as Deities was largely forgotten by the majority of the population as they followed the Christ-God brought by Patrick to Ireland. Only those who would see them honour them – and in return, are honoured by them. It could be argued that the Old Gods gifted the artists and writers of the Irish and Scottish Literary revivals the blessing of seeing them walk the earth again, even though this may have brought problems on a human level. O'Sullivan was a drinker. One can only wonder if the cause of this was, in part, due to the tensions he may have felt living with such fundamental differences in perception with the bulk of the population.

Credo is O'Sullivan's moment of seeing clearly, seeing – from his own position – what was there and not what others would wish him to see. He saw Angus, his living God. It is this clarity of vision that links to Yeats's *The Collar-Bone of a Hare.* Both men share a moment where personal revelation on their paths were uncomfortable and placed them at odds with other people's thoughts.

Pathworking with these Poems

Seeing clearly is the intent and the focus of using these two poems in Pathworking. The Pathworking should lead to a clearer understanding of self and those things that must be let go if you are to progress on your chosen path. This is a Pathworking that works best outdoors.

Meditation Tools

If possible, find a stone or a bone with a naturally occurring hole through it and have the symbol of the triple spiral about your person. The spiral is not only a tool to help you walk the worlds, it is a protection that will always help you return to the centre, to where you are, if you follow its flowing lines.

Yeats pierced the hole in the hare bone of his poem. However, Yeats was an adept of the Golden Dawn and more than ready to force himself to see the path he needed to take to achieve what he wanted in his life. In short, he knew what he was doing and he knew how to walk between the worlds safely. For those less familiar with this, it may be better to go with the flow of the spiral and see what happens naturally, without forcing the issue. However, experienced Pathwalkers, who have the necessary knowledge to circumvent potential problems that may arise from trying to force a contact with the Otherworld, may prefer to emulate Yeats's actions, if so wished.

Pathworking

Find a quiet place where the three realms of the land, sea and sky meet, a beautiful place with trees, water and sky. Make libations to the Guardians of the space you have chosen, asking their permission to Pathwork. You will know it is safe to do so; your answer will come to you – perhaps on the wind, perhaps in the appearance of an animal that is curious about you. However, should the answer be no, find another place.

Once you have the acceptance of the place chosen, you are

ready to begin your Pathworking. Cast your circle and prepare your protection. Then sit quietly, holding your seeing stone as you contemplate the meanings and ideas at the heart of both poems. Let your mind wander into the lives of O'Sullivan and Yeats, feel what they felt when they wrote those words. Consider the clarity of vision within their works. Breathe slowly and deeply as you do so, feel yourself moving into the hearts of the poets.

Hold on to the connection made with the poems. Picture the spiral. See it begin to move as energy, as life force flows through its whorls and branches and back again to the centre, to move in another direction. Call to Angus and request permission to place yourself at the centre of the spiral, in his protection. Ask his help in seeing your path. Angus will answer you if your intent is clear and honest. He will invite you into the unmoving centre of the pulsating spiral. You will be Angus-blessed and the emotional intensity of this feeling cannot be understated. Many find it too intense and difficult to cope with. Be brave and accept the gift of his protection when he offers it to you. Stand in the centre, feel the bliss of Angus' love flow through you as you watch the spirals turn. Enjoy the moment.

When it feels like the right time, lift your seeing stone to your eye and look through it. Watch closely as you are shown the possibilities of the spiral of your own life. Look in the moment, accept what you see, note the sounds, animals, people and landscapes – do not try to analyse it; that is a task for later. Should you be invited to participate in any activity, politely decline. You stand in the centre with Angus as an observer, not a participant. You seek clarity of vision and guidance on your own path. Do not be pulled into a possibility you have not had time to consider back in this world.

The visions will fade naturally and you will find yourself back at the centre of the spiral, with Angus. Thank him as a God and a benefactor; acknowledge the honour he has paid you by his protection and guidance.

Slowly return to this world. Allow your breathing to return to normal and let your body wake up from this intense experience. It may take a short while for you to feel as if you are completely in this realm, this is normal after such an intense interaction with Angus. When you feel entirely yourself, conduct your usual rites and uncast your circle.

You are now in a position to contemplate the meanings of your Pathworking visions and to explore them in your journal. It is likely that you will experience serendipity over the following weeks as the answers to your request for clarity come to you. You will know what needs to be let go and what has to be cherished in order to develop your spirituality. You will have used Yeats's poem to show you this. But you will also have used O'Sullivan's poem to connect directly to Angus, to Deity; and you will have done so without the intercession of a third party. That in itself is a valuable lesson about the experiential nature of Pagan spirituality.

Conclusion

This short book is a very simple overview of a method of Pathworking that might help enhance personal practice. I hope it has enabled some, who may not have considered this approach before, to realise the potential poetry has to teach us about our Paths, our Gods and ourselves.

May the messages from the hearts of the poets touch your heart and bless you with their understandings.

Acknowledgement

My thanks to Mrs Frances Sommerville for her kind permission to use Seumas O'Sullivan's poem, *Credo*.

Endnotes

1. The calendar changed in the 18th C and 11 days were lost from the year 1752. In that year, people went to bed on September 2nd and woke up on September 14th. This caused some concern and confusion at the time, but in the more temperate regions of southern Britain it is likely this fast-forwarding of 11 days had no real effect. However, this is arguably not the case in Scotland, where seasons tend to come several weeks behind their southern neighbour anyway and fast-forwarding days certainly didn't mean that nature was going to oblige by pretending seasons were any earlier. In addition, Celtic tribes counted the day differently – the new day began when the sun set, therefore twilight was one day merging into another. It is worth considering the effects of the artificial measurements of seasons imposed by the calendar and the days when we chose to honour our Gods and Goddesses. Indeed, Ireland still has remnants of Lughnasadah celebrations, timed by the old calendar, in the Puck Fair, held annually in Killorglin, Kerry on the 10th, 11th and 12th of August.

2. Donald A. MacKenzie, 'The Coming of Angus and Bride', *Scottish Wonder Tales from Myth and Legend*, (New York: Frederick A. Stokes, 1917, NY: Dover Publications, 1997, pp. 33-49.)

3. MacLeod, Fiona, 'The Gaelic Heart', *The Winged Destiny: Studies in the Spiritual History of the Gael*, (London: Heinemann, 1910, 1913, 1920, p. 209.)

4. Young, Ella, 'The Earth Shapers, *Celtic Wonder Tales*, (Dublin: Maunsel & Co, 1910, NY: Dover, 1995, pp. 3-11.)

5. MacLeod, Fiona, 'The Awakening of Angus Og', *The Winged Destiny: Studies in the Spiritual History of the Gael*, (London: Heinemann, 1910, 1913, 1920, pp. 91-99.)

6. *The Corries* version of *Dream Angus* is a beautiful example of this lullaby (available on *Youtube.*)
7. *Register of the Privy Council*, Edinburgh, 3rd S. VI p.210.
8. Hebrews, 4:12

Moon Books invites you to begin or deepen your encounter with Paganism, in all its rich, creative, flourishing forms.

9781780992853